Peachy Pickings:
Favorite Recipes from
Livesay Orchards

Collected by Livesay Orchards
Porter, Oklahoma 1966-2016

Copyright © 2016 Livesay Orchards
Porter, Oklahoma

All rights reserved. No part of this book may be reproduced without express permission.

www.samsonpublishingcompany.com

Samson Publishing Company LLC

ISBN-13: 978-0692743430
ISBN-10: 069274343X

A special thanks to Liz McMahon and the Wagoner County Historical Society for helping us track down some of the historical pictures included in this book and to Geraldine Dilbeck, who has kept perhaps every news article published about Porter in the last few decades and let us comb through her collection for facts about the town's peach-growing history.

Food photography on pages 9, 39, 55 and 65 credited to Courtney McBride Photography.

CONTENTS

1 The Porter Peach Story   2

2 The Livesay Family Story   4

3 Peach Recipes   11

4 Apple Recipes   41

5 Pumpkin Recipes   57

6 Farm Friendly Recipes   67

7 Index   86

PREFACE

In 1966, Austin Livesay bought an existing peach orchard in Porter, Oklahoma, making our family the newest members in an already-successful farming tradition. Today, fifty years later, we have grown and diversified the original farming operation, but have remained true to our agricultural heritage. This collection of tried and true recipes from our family, as well as some from a handful of our long-time neighbors, are our favorite ways to enjoy the fruits of our labors. It is our hope that these recipes will become part of your family's traditions as well.

The Livesay Family

THE PORTER PEACH STORY

To many people in Oklahoma, the term "Porter Peaches" is synonymous with hot summer days and juicy, ripe peaches. It is often misunderstood that a Porter Peach is a specific type or variety of peach. However, the term simply refers to a peach grown in Porter, Oklahoma, a small rural community in northeast Oklahoma.

Peaches have been grown in Porter since before statehood. The fertile farm ground between the Verdigris and the Arkansas River was the perfect backdrop for growing peaches and other crops. Originally part of the Creek Nation Allotment, the community of Porter and the surrounding areas boasted some of the most prosperous farms in Indian Territory, including the farm of Ben Marshall. The son of a wealthy and influential mixed-blood Creek, Marshall attended the Carlisle Indian Industrial School in Pennsylvania. It was during his years at Carlisle that Marshall first learned about fruit production, working during summer breaks for a Pennsylvania farmer who owned peach and apple orchards. When Marshall returned to the Creek allotments in Indian Territory in 1890, he planted the first commercial peach orchard in the area, five miles southeast of the town of Porter.

The orchard gained national attention in 1904, when Marshall took his peaches to the Louisiana Purchase Exposition in St. Louis. Marshall's peaches received high praise at the World's Fair, winning Marshall and the first Porter Peaches a Gold Medal for quality.

A grocery store in Muskogee, Oklahoma with peaches brought from Porter to sell in 1939

Dr. Mike Smith, OSU horticulturist and his wife, selecting the Prize Peaches from the 1974 Porter Peach Festival.

Peaches, apples, and other fruits and vegetables remained a mainstay in the Porter economy into the next century. At one time, Porter boasted eight concurrently operated commercial peach orchards, earning the distinction as Oklahoma's official Peach Capital. In 1967, the inaugural Porter Peach Festival was held to showcase the town's unique economic boon. While most of these early orchards have faded into the pages of history, Porter continues to produce the majority of the state's peaches and celebrates the continuing legacy of the early farmers every July at the annual Peach Festival.

Local musicians perform at a Porter Peach Festival in the 1980s.

THE LIVESAY FAMILY STORY

Like many families in America, our story is made up of men and women who worked the land. In fact, from 1729 to present day, from Lancashire, England through Virginia, Tennessee, Arkansas, Texas, and finally into Indian Territory, our ancestors, without fail, listed their profession as farmers or ranchers.

A Peach Orchard in Porter

It was this connection to the land that drew Austin Livesay to Porter. Born in Tuskegee, Oklahoma in 1910, Austin trained to be an electrician in Chicago before returning home to Oklahoma. In the 1940s, while out working on an electrical job in the area, Austin learned of a 462-acre farm in Porter that was for sale. The land was rich and fertile, and Austin knew that it would be a good place to put down roots and farm. Unfortunately, Austin couldn't come up with the down payment and the farm was sold to Sam Denison, who planted peach and apple orchards on the land.

Austin Livesay, the founder of Livesay Orchards

Still determined to farm, Austin purchased some land in Broken Arrow where he grew cotton, soybeans, and wheat. Twenty years passed before Austin got word that the farm he wanted in Porter was once again for sale. In the fall of 1966, Austin purchased the farm he had wanted years before, but now it boasted approximately 55 acres of peach and 45 acres of apple orchards.

Mr. and Mrs. Sam Denison and their children sitting on the porch of their "comfortable farm home" three miles southwest of Porter (the white house today). Taken by Louis Reed on May 26, 1947.

An Unplanned Peach Grower

Austin soon learned that growing peaches and apples was far different than growing cotton. The fruit trees required year-round care and all the harvesting was (and still is) done by hand, and then had to be quickly sold to the public. Growing peaches brought new risks as well. In Oklahoma, one late freeze or a late spring hail storm can wipe out a summer harvest in the space of just a few minutes. Despite these new challenges, Austin was determined to make a go of this new venture and set about to learn all he could about these crops.

Austin harvested his first peach and apple crop in the summer/fall of 1967 and asked his nephew, David Livesay, to help him with that first harvest. Regrettably, Austin's life as a peach grower was short-lived. After just two years on the farm he had wanted for so long, Austin suffered a heart attack out working in the orchard in January of 1969 and passed away shortly after.

After Austin's death, C.D. Livesay, Austin's brother and David's father, acquired ownership of the farm in Porter, and in 1970 David and his wife Madeline, along with their young sons Kent and Steve, moved to Porter to live on and operate the farm full-time. In the following decades, the farming operation continued to expand and evolve. Neighboring farms and orchards were purchased, the original open-air market was expanded, and additional acreage for field and fruit crops was leased and farmed as neighboring land owners saw our commitment to the land and community.

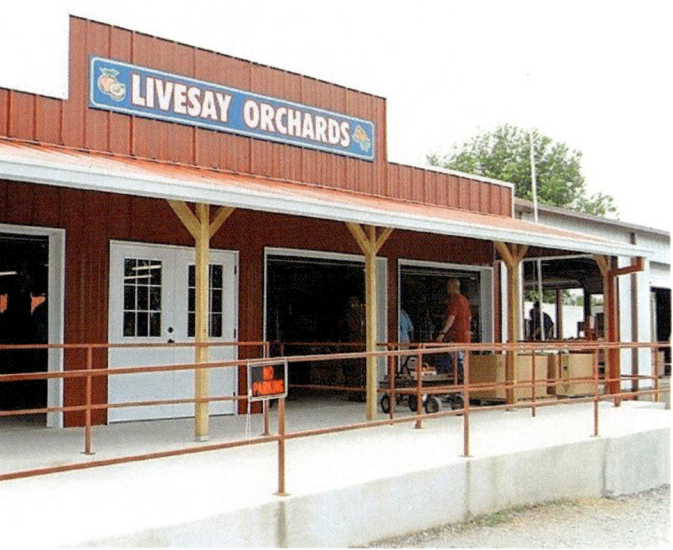

Our open air market, circa early 1980s

The market today . . . still open air!

A New Generation's Commitment to the Land

Today, Livesay Farms & Orchards is owned and operated by Kent and Steve Livesay and their families. The orchards are the largest in the state, with approximately 140 acres of peaches and 15 acres of apples – just over 11,000 trees. In addition to the peach and apple orchards, other fruits and vegetables, including nectarines, watermelons, cantaloupes, pumpkins, squash, tomatoes, okra, sweet corn, and blackberries are grown and sold in our market. Fruit and vegetable production in Oklahoma can be risky and in order to survive, farmers must make sure their eggs aren't all in one basket. To provide an additional source of income and hedge against years that the peaches freeze, we grow row crops such as wheat, soybeans, field corn, and grain sorghum, which make up the majority of our acres under cultivation. We also run a small herd of cattle on pasture land – because farms should just have cows! In recent years, we have expanded our school tours, providing an opportunity for local elementary schools and groups to visit the farm and educate children and their families on how apples and pumpkins are grown. During weekends in the fall, the farm is buzzing with families visiting to pick apples and visit the pumpkin patch.

There is an old hymn that rings true to us here on the farm:

• • •

We plow the fields, and scatter the good seed on the land,
But it is fed and watered by God's almighty hand;
He sends the snow in winter, the warmth to swell the grain,
The breezes and the sunshine, and soft refreshing rain.
All good gifts around us are sent from heaven above,
Then thank the Lord, O thank the Lord for all His love.

"We Plow the Fields", Matthias Claudius,
translated by Jane M. Campbell

• • •

Farming can be a difficult life. The hours are long, the work is hard, and often success is dependent on factors outside of our control. But farming is also a blessed life, a life that very quickly teaches dependence on God and awareness of His goodness. We are thankful for the opportunity we have had to be stewards of this land and plan on being here growing and selling our crops for at least fifty years to come!

Through the years, we have been blessed to have many folks who double as not just great friends and neighbors, but also employees. On a farm like this, there is never a shortage of work, and we could not grow and harvest our crops without the help of our year-round and seasonal employees. Whether it's an employee that has been around for decades or a high school student earning his first paycheck, everyone plays a necessary role in getting the fruits of our labors into the hands of our loyal customers. In addition to the folks you see and talk to when you come down to buy your peaches or pick out your pumpkins, there are numerous people that have put in long hours planting, tending, harvesting, and preparing crops for purchase.

There is no way we could mention everyone who has contributed to the success of the farm through the years (and we obviously don't take enough pictures!). But, we are so thankful for each and every one of them and cherish the memories we have of them.

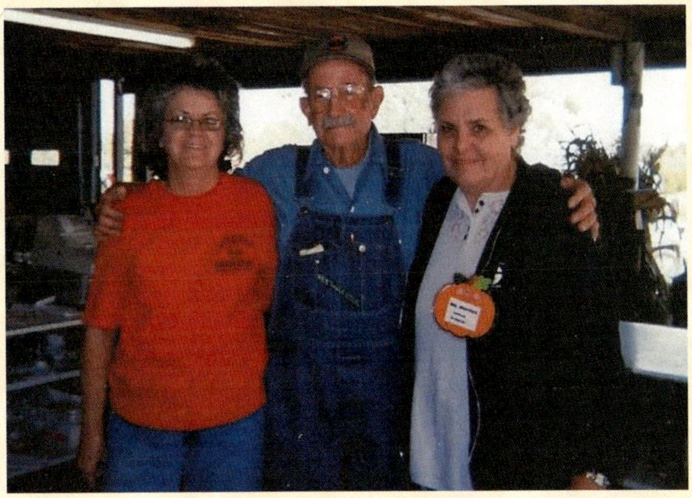
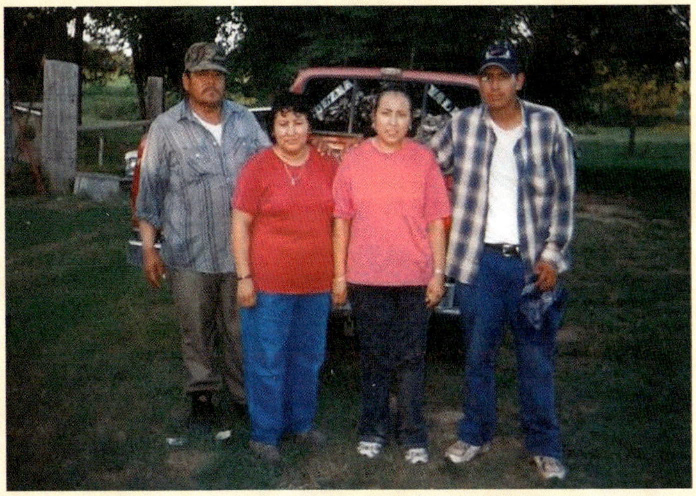
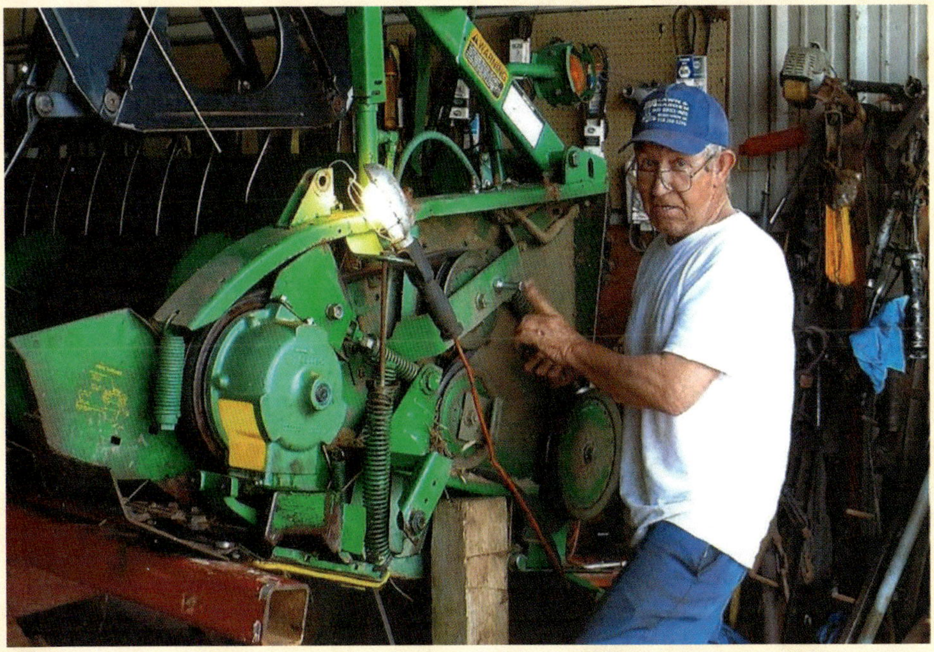
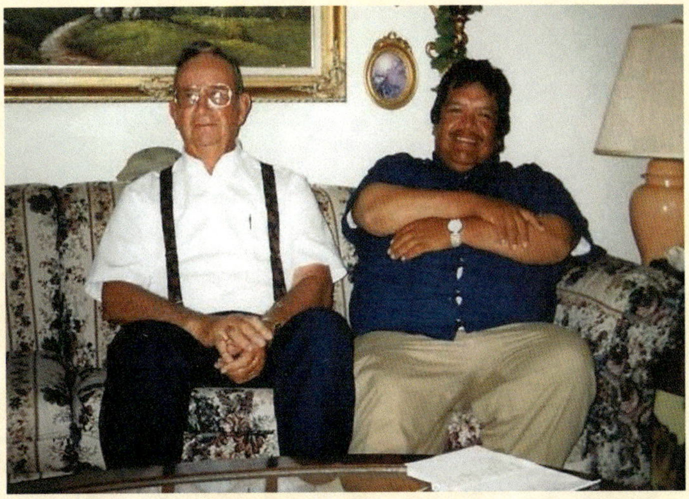
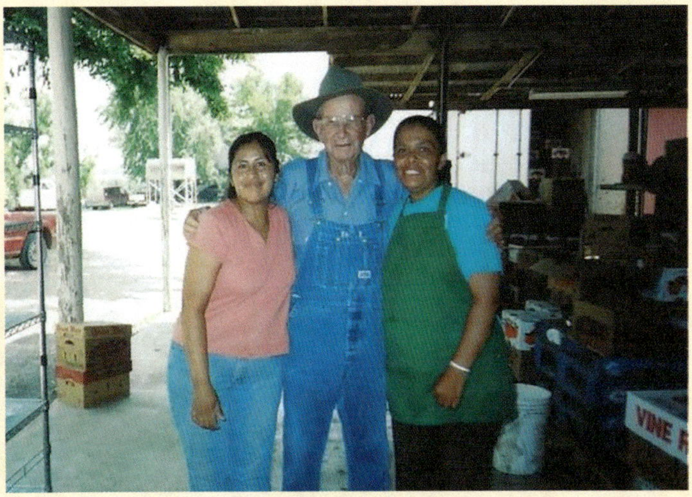

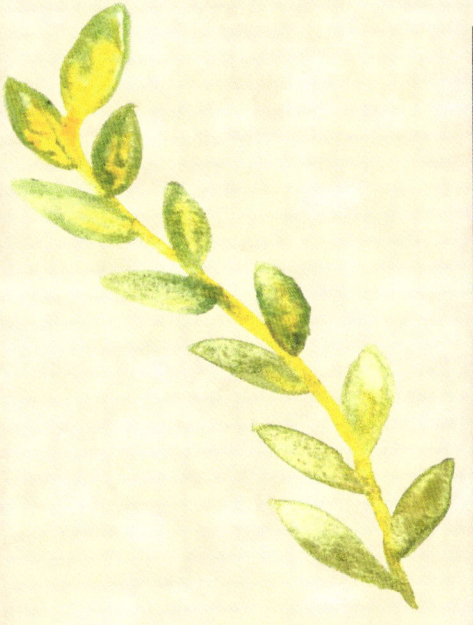

Pictured are: Peach Crumble (pg 13), Creamy Peach Pie (pg 23), Peach Iced Tea (pg 13), Honey Peach Butter (pg 11)

PEACH RECIPES

An apple is an excellent thing –

until you have tried a peach.

George de Maurier

HONEY PEACH BUTTER
Brenda Livesay (Steve's wife)

10 pounds of peaches, peeled and chopped (approximately an 8 qt box or peck)
½ cup water
4 ½ cups sugar
1 ½ cups honey

In a large kettle, cook the peaches in water until soft. Press through a sieve or food mill. Measure 12 cups pulp; return to kettle. Add sugar and honey. Cook, stirring often, until mixture thickens, about 1 ¼ hours. Stir more frequently as it thickens to prevent sticking. Pour hot into hot jars, leaving ¼ in. headspace. Place hot canning lids onto jar and adjust the cap lid until tight. Process jars for 10 minutes in a boiling-water bath.

Yield: 6 pints

PEACH FREEZER JAM
Dawna Livesay (Kent's wife)

4 cups peeled, crushed fresh peaches
¼ cup fresh strained lemon juice
1 cup light corn syrup
1 package (1 ¾ oz.) powdered fruit pectin
5 ½ cups sugar

Measure peaches into a large kettle; add lemon juice. While stirring with a wooden spoon, slowly add the pectin. Let stand 20 minutes; stir every 5 minutes to blend pectin with fruit. Add syrup and blend well; add sugar and blend well. Cook over low heat to about 100 degrees, just warm to the touch. Do not allow mixture to become hot. Pour jam into jars to within ½ inch of top. Cover jars at once. Let stand until jelly consistency. Store in freezer until ready to use. Store in refrigerator once jar has been opened.

Yields: About 8 half-pint jars

PEACH JALAPEÑO PEPPER JELLY

Melanie Warren (Steve and Brenda's daughter)

6 medium jalapeño peppers
1 medium green bell pepper
1 medium red bell pepper
1 ½ cup apple cider vinegar
1 tablespoon crushed red pepper flakes
6 ½ cups sugar
2 pouches Certo liquid pectin
1 cup diced peaches

Wash, seed, and dice the peppers. I like to use a food processor so they get pretty finely diced. Finely dice the peeled fresh peaches. In a large stockpot, combine peppers, sugar, vinegar, and crushed red pepper flakes over high heat (you can leave out the red pepper flakes if you want a milder jelly). Cook until you reach a full rolling boil. Boil for five minutes. Add pectin and peaches and return to a full rolling boil for three minutes. Let the jelly cool for a minute and skim off foam. Place in hot jars. Process in a water bath canner for 10 minutes.

Yield: 7 half pints

Recipe Notes

This Peach Pepper Jelly is one of the go-to condiments in my fridge. Use it as a simple appetizer that will always get rave reviews: just pour it over a block of cream cheese and serve with crackers. Or, mix it with some honey (and sometimes I add spicy mustard) and use it to glaze chicken or pork to grill or roast. It also makes a wonderful dressing over a salad of fresh summer vegetables and grilled or poached chicken. To make a Peach Pepper Vinaigrette just add minced garlic (1 clove) and fresh lime juice (one lime or about 3 tablespoons) to 1/4 cup of the Peach Pepper Jelly. Then add however much oil needed to thin it to the consistency you want.

Melanie

PEACH MELBA FLOAT
Dawna Livesay

3 peeled, sliced peaches
1 banana, sliced
1 pint raspberry sherbet
Ginger Ale

Arrange peach slices, banana slices, and a scoop of sherbet in stemmed glasses and set in freezer to frost. Fill glasses with ginger ale and serve with spoons and straws.

Yield: 6 glasses

MEL'S FAMOUS PEACH MILKSHAKES
Melanie Warren

2 peeled, sliced peaches (fresh or frozen)
½ cup whole milk
4 healthy scoops of vanilla ice cream
6 oz. of peach nectar (I prefer the Jumex brand which you can usually find in the ethnic aisle of grocery stores)

Puree peaches in blender until smooth. Add the rest of the ingredients and process until smooth and creamy. Before pouring out, check the taste and consistency. Add more ice cream to make it thicker, or milk to thin it out. Additional peach nectar can be added for sweetness, if needed. Serve with whipped cream and maraschino cherries!

Yield: 4 glasses

PEACH SLUSH
Dawna Livesay

2 cups of peaches, cold or partially frozen
½ cup powdered sugar
1 6-oz. can frozen concentrate lemonade

Place all of the above ingredients in a blender; fill to the top with ice. Crush until slushy. (This is a great recipe to use frozen peaches in – it's best with those barely thawed peaches!)

Yield: 6 glasses

PEACH ICED TEA
Melanie Warren

1 cup sugar
8 cups water, divided
2-3 sliced fresh peaches
3 tea bags

Optional: Lemonade

Bring the sugar, peaches, and 1 cup of water to a boil. Reduce heat to medium and stir the mixture until the sugar dissolves, crushing the peach slices as you stir. Remove from heat, cover, and let sit for 30 minutes.

Meanwhile, boil 7 cups of water and brew tea, letting steep for about 5 minutes. Remove tea bags and refrigerate.

Strain the peach syrup through a strainer to remove the fruit pieces. Add the syrup to tea and serve over ice. I like to add ½ gallon of prepared lemonade to this peach tea and serve it as a "Peachy Arnold Palmer"!

Yield: ½ gallon of tea or 1 gallon of Peachy Arnold Palmer

PRESERVING PEACHES

Nothing beats a peach pie in the dead of winter . . . so preserving some peaches to get you through the cold winter days is a must! Peaches can be canned, dried, or frozen. Here on the farm, we are partial to freezing. It's easy and the peaches retain a great flavor. See our tips below on enjoying peaches after the season is over.

Freezing Peach Slices

- Peel and slice fresh peaches.
- Treat with ascorbic acid (Fruit Fresh) to prevent the fruit from browning. Mix together so that the Fruit Fresh gets evenly distributed.
- Place the peaches in a good quality freezer bag, filling about ¾ of the way full.
- Make sure to remove all the extra air and seal up tight.

Ready to Go Peach Pie Filling

- When you're freezing your peaches you can leave them plain, like described above, or add sugar to taste.
- Make peach pie filling and freez the correct amount for a pie in a freezer bag, and then defrost as you have a craving for Porter Peach Pie during the winter months.
- Just make sure you label appropriately – Melanie has been known to double-sugar a pie because she forgot she had pre-sugared!

Freezing Peaches Whole

- Don't have time to peel and slice peaches during the summer? We know the feeling. We wash peaches and then place the whole peaches on a cookie sheet or pan in the freezer. When they are completely frozen, transfer them to a ziplock bag.
- Defrost the desired amount at room temperature for about 3 – 4 hours. If you let these peaches completely thaw, they will be a little mushy, BUT these slightly icy peaches are great in cottage cheese, milkshakes, smoothies, or ice cream!

PEACH MUFFINS
Brenda Livesay

Dry Ingredients:
- *1 ½ cups all-purpose flour*
- *¾ tsp. salt*
- *1 cup sugar*
- *½ tsp. baking soda*
- *½ tsp. cinnamon*
- *¼ tsp nutmeg*

2 eggs
½ cup vegetable oil
½ tsp vanilla
¼ tsp almond extract
1 ¼ cup chopped fresh peaches
½ cup chopped pecans (or nut of your choice)
Cinnamon/sugar mixture (optional)

Combine all the dry ingredients in a mixing bowl. Make a well in center of dry ingredients. In a separate container, beat the vegetable oil and eggs together well. Add the oil and eggs to the dry ingredients and stir only until the dry ingredients are moistened. Stir in peaches, vanilla, almond extract, and nuts. Put approximately 1/3 cup of the batter in paper lined muffin tins. If desired, sprinkle a little cinnamon/sugar mixture on top of muffin before baking. Bake at 350 degrees for 20-25 minutes.

Yield: 12 muffins

Recipe Notes

Here's a baking hint. This muffin recipe is a "quick bread". Leave the electric mixer in the cabinet! Quick breads should be mixed only with a spoon by hand. If you stir this type of bread too fast or too much, your finished product will probably be tough.   Brenda

You can also use this recipe to make peach bread by spooning it into a well-greased 9 inch loaf pan. Bake the loaf at 350 degrees for 1 hour.

PEACH POUND CAKE
Brenda Livesay

1 cup butter or margarine, softened
3 cups sugar
6 eggs, room temperature
3 cups flour
¼ teaspoon baking soda
¾ teaspoon salt
½ cup sour cream, room temperature
2 cups finely chopped, peeled peaches
1 teaspoon vanilla
1 teaspoon almond extract

Cream butter and sugar together until light and fluffy. Add eggs one at a time, mixing after each addition. Combine flour, soda and salt together. Mix sour cream and peaches together. Add dry ingredients to creamed mixture alternately with peach mixture. Stir in vanilla and almond extract. Bake at 350 degrees in a greased and floured 10 inch tube pan or bundt pan for 70-80 minutes. You could also divide the batter into two 9-inch loaf pans and bake for 1 hour. Remove from pans to cool after 10 minutes. When completely cooled, dust with powdered sugar.

PEACHES AND CREAM CAKE
Andrea Parnell (Longtime employee and friend)

1 yellow or white cake mix
8 Porter Peaches, peeled, sliced and dipped in Fruit Fresh
½ cup sugar
8 oz. carton of cool whip
1 box instant vanilla pudding

Bake cake as directed and allow to cool. Cut into 2 inch squares. Add sugar to the peaches and stir. Place half the cake squares in a large bowl. Mix vanilla pudding as directed on box. Spread half the pudding over the cake squares. Put half the peaches and sugar mixture over the pudding. Spread half the carton of Cool Whip over the peaches. Repeat the layering process. Leave a few peach slices to go on top. Arrange peach slices on top.

Refrigerate and enjoy!

Yield: 16 servings

PEACH AND BLUEBERRY COFFEE CAKE

Melanie Warren

1 ½ cups flour
1 teaspoon baking powder
½ teaspoon baking soda
¼ cup butter, softened
1 cup sugar
2 eggs
½ teaspoon vanilla
½ cup Greek yogurt
2 peaches, sliced (I like to keep the skins on for color but you can peel if you want)
6 oz. blueberries
1 teaspoon granulated sugar
1 teaspoon Fruit Fresh
Powdered sugar

Grease the sides and bottom of a 9x3 spring-form pan. Cut a circle out of parchment paper to line the bottom of the pan and grease that well, too. You can use a regular cake pan instead; it's just harder to get out pretty!

Sift flour, baking powder, and baking soda together. In a separate bowl, beat butter, sugar, and 2 eggs until very light and fluffy, about 3 minutes or so on high speed. Add vanilla and Greek yogurt and continue beating until very creamy and light in color – about 1 more minute.

Mix the flour mixture in, with the mixer speed down low. Mix until just combined – do not overmix! Pour the cake mix into the greased pan. Scatter sliced peaches and blueberries evenly over the top of the cake. Sprinkle fruit with sugar and Fruit Fresh.

Bake at 350 degrees for about an hour until the cake is golden in color and the cake is cooked through in the middle. Let the cake cool (still in the pan) on a wire rack for about an hour. After it's cooled down, you can release the sides of the pan and slide the parchment paper and the cake onto a cake stand. Sift some powdered sugar over the top of the cake.

Because of the yogurt, this cake needs to be served the day you make it or the day after. Any longer than that and it will get kind of soggy. Keep it in the refrigerator to keep it fresh that next day.

Peachy WEDNESDAY

The news about peaches is peachy. This year's crop is the best in years. Juicy, sweet peaches– according to a survey the third most popular fruit in the country– from Porter will be available in Tulsa markets for the next few weeks. They're also available on trees at Porter if you want to pick your own.

For a collection of peach-dish recipes with a definite Oklahoma accent see the Living Section of Wednesday's Tulsa World. One of the recipes is for Peach Melba using luscious, fat blackberries, also in season now.

Check tomorrow's World for news that affects you, your family and your community. For convenient home delivery of your World, call 582-0921.

TULSA WORLD
Building a Bett...

Uncle Rufus Blair, Madeline's brother-in-law, was a much-beloved fixture at Livesay Orchards for decades. Retired from the military, Rufus started helping out at the farm in the mid-1970s. Rufus loved people and he loved selling peaches, both at the open air market and at the pick-your-own stand down at the corner orchard. Always one to spin a good tale, customers old and new alike felt like family after visiting with Uncle Rufus. Even when his family insisted he slow down, Rufus would make the drive down to the orchard, sitting on the red tables right inside the market where he could greet everyone as they came in and make sure they left with enough peaches to go home and make a peach pie (though, he assured them, his wife, Virginia, made the best). The farm's just not the same without Uncle Rufus, but the lessons we learned from him live on.

PEACH CRISP
Brenda Livesay

8 cups sliced fresh peaches
1 cup regular sugar, or to taste, depending on sweetness of fruit
2 tablespoons cornstarch
1 teaspoon cinnamon
¼ teaspoon nutmeg

Topping:
1 cup packed brown sugar
1 cup flour
½ cup quick oats, uncooked
1 teaspoon cinnamon
2/3 cup margarine, softened

Slice peaches into a 13x9 pan. Mix the regular sugar, cornstarch, 1 tsp cinnamon, and nutmeg together in a bowl and sprinkle over the peaches in the pan.

Place all the topping ingredients together in a bowl and mix until crumbly. Put the crumb mixture over peaches. Bake at 400 degrees for 45 minutes. Serve warm with ice cream or whipped topping

Everyone gets in on the work at a family farm. Above are Steve and Brenda's kids, Brian and Melanie, circa 1995. To the left are Kent and Dawna's boys, Kyle and Nathan, circa 2005.

PEACH DESSERT ENCHILADAS

Kaylee Herriman (Cousin a few times removed of Brenda; also Kaylee's mom, Karen, worked at the orchard for a few years)
Peach Festival Dessert Winner

2 8-oz. tubes of crescent rolls
2 sticks butter
1 ½ cups sugar
1 teaspoon cinnamon
4 firm Livesay Orchards peaches, peeled and quartered
12 oz. can of Mountain Dew

Melt butter; add sugar and cinnamon. Unroll crescent dough and place one peach quarter on each crescent. Roll dough around peach from large end to small. Place in 12x10x2 inch plan. Pour butter mixture over the rolls and then pour Mountain Dew on top. Bake at 350 degrees for 45 minutes.

Yield: 16 servings

PEACH ROLL UPS

Phyllis Parnell (Andrea's mother-in-law, occasional employee, and renowned local cook!)

8 oz. cream cheese, softened
1 cup fresh peaches, finely chopped
½ teaspoon vanilla
½ cup powdered sugar
8 flour tortillas

Blend cream cheese, powdered sugar, peaches, and vanilla until creamy. Spread on flour tortillas. Wrap each tortilla in plastic wrap and refrigerate several hours.

Remove the plastic wrap and cut in slices (1/2 inch or so) or you can serve whole.

PEACH CRUMBLE

Melanie Warren

6 cups sliced peaches, sprinkled with Fruit Fresh
¼ cup packed brown sugar
1 cup plus 3 tablespoons flour, divided
½ teaspoon ground cinnamon
1 cup sugar
1 teaspoon baking powder
¼ teaspoon salt
¼ teaspoon ground nutmeg
1 large egg, lightly beaten
1 stick butter, melted

Place peaches in a greased shallow baking dish. In a small bowl, combine brown sugar, 3 tablespoons of flour, and cinnamon; sprinkle over the peaches. Combine the remaining flour, sugar, baking powder, salt, and nutmeg. Stir in egg until the mixture resembles coarse crumbs. Sprinkle over the peaches. Pour butter evenly over the dish. Bake for 35 – 40 minutes at 375 degrees. Serve warm with ice cream!

Phyllis Parnell, peeling some Porter peaches for one of her many wonderful desserts!

GLAZED PEACH PIE
Brenda Livesay

1 cup sugar
¼ cup cornstarch
Dash of nutmeg
½ teaspoon cinnamon
2 tablespoons water
1 tablespoon lemon juice
2 ½ cups pureed peeled fresh peaches
3 ½ cups sliced peeled fresh peaches
1 pie pastry (9 inches); baked

In a saucepan, combine sugar, cornstarch, salt, nutmeg, and cinnamon. Stir in water, lemon juice, and pureed peaches. Cook mixture over medium heat, stirring constantly (about 5 minutes), until mixture is thickened. Pour all but ½ cup of glaze into the pie shell. Top with sliced peaches and brush with reserved glaze. Chill for at least 3 hours.

Yield: 8 servings

FRESH PEACH PIE
Brenda Livesay

1 cup sugar
2 tablespoons cornstarch
1 cup water
1 package (3 ounces) peach-flavored gelatin
3 cups sliced peeled ripe peaches
1 pastry shell (9 inch) baked or a graham cracker crust
Whipped cream, optional

In a saucepan, combine sugar, cornstarch, and water until smooth. Cook and stir over medium heat until bubbly and thickened. Remove from the heat; stir in gelatin until dissolved. Let the gelatin mixture cool for awhile. (Let it cool while you are peeling your peaches, this way your peaches will not have time to turn brown while you are cooking the gelatin mixture). Arrange the peeled peaches in crust; pour the gelatin filling over the peaches. Chill until set, about 2 hours. Serve with whipped cream if desired.

Yield: 6-8 servings

FOOLPROOF PIECRUST
Brenda Livesay

Cut together:
4 cups plus 1 tablespoon flour
1 ¾ cups shortening
1 tablespoon sugar
2 teaspoons salt

Mix together:
½ cup cold water
1 egg
1 tablespoon white vinegar

Mix the water mixture with the flour/shortening mixture <u>by hand</u>. Mix only until moistened well and easily forms into a large ball. Do this gently. "Tough" piecrust is usually caused by overworking the dough. Place in a covered bowl and chill in refrigerator at least 15 minutes before rolling into desired shape. Dough can be left in fridge up to 1 week. I generally like to make the pie crust dough the day before I make pies. This allows plenty of time for the dough to be chilled which makes it easier to handle. This recipe makes enough crust for two double crust 9-inch pies.

PEACH AND BLACKBERRY PIE
Melanie Warren

2 cups diced peaches, sprinkled with Fruit Fresh
1 cup blackberries
½ cup sugar
¼ cup brown sugar
2 tablespoons cornstarch
1 teaspoon ground cloves
¼ teaspoon nutmeg
1/8 teaspoon almond extract
Foolproof Piecrust

In a large bowl, combine the peaches, blackberries, and sugars. Toss gently. I like to let that stand and meld together for a bit while I roll out the pie dough (prepared and chilled according to directions).

Assemble your pie with a bottom and top crust and bake for 15 minutes at 425 degrees. Reduce heat to 375 degrees and continue baking another 35 minutes, until crust is golden brown. Cool pie on a wire rack for three hours before serving.

Yield: 6-8 servings

Quick and Easy Hand Pies

Mom's Foolproof Piecrust recipe is truly foolproof - even I can do it! It's pretty impossible to beat homemade pie crust, but for those days when you want to serve pie for dinner and just don't have time for pie crust, whip up a batch of Puff Pastry Hand Pies! Thaw out two sheets of frozen puff pastry dough. Find something that is about a 3-inch circle - the top of a glass, a cookie cutter, or I use an old biscuit cutter I inherited. Roll out the dough so that you can get 12 circles out of each sheet (you might have to cut some, and then gather the leftover dough and reroll it to get the last few circles). Place 12 of the pastry circles on a greased cookie sheet. Put a heaping tablespoon or so of any prepared pie filling you want on each pastry circle. Top with the remaining pastry circles. Use a fork to seal the edges together, crimping them along the sides to be pretty. In a small bowl, beat one egg and use a pastry brush to brush the egg on the top of each little pie. Cut one or two little slits in the top of each pie and bake in a 400 degree oven for around 16 - 18 minutes.

Melanie

CREAMY PEACH PIE
Brenda Livesay

1 package (3 ounces) peach-flavored gelatin
2/3 cup boiling water
1 cup vanilla ice cream
1 carton (8 ounces) frozen whipped topping, thawed
1 ½ cups diced fresh, peeled peaches
1 deep-dish pastry shell that has been baked or a graham cracker crust
Sliced peaches, mint (optional)

In a large bowl, dissolve gelatin in boiling water; stir in ice cream until melted and smooth. This is easier to mix if you let the ice cream soften some before putting it in the gelatin mixture. Add whipped topping and mix well. Fold in diced peaches. Pour into pastry shell. Chill until firm, about 3 hours. If desired, garnish with sliced peaches that have been sprinkled with Fruit Fresh to prevent them from turning brown, and/or fresh mint leaves.

Recipe Notes

Our family likes this recipe just as well without any sort of crust. We sometimes put the peach mixture in dessert cups and then sprinkle a few graham cracker crumbs on top. Saves on calories too! **Brenda**

I've also served this recipe in individual graham cracker crusts, in waffle cone bowls, in bowls made out of phyllo crust... The possibilities are endless but always delicious! **Melanie**

PEACH JELLO PIE
Phyllis Parnell (Andrea's mother-in-law, occasional employee, and renowned local cook!)

Graham cracker pie crust

Cream Layer:
  1 (8 oz.) package cream cheese
  1 cup powdered sugar
  1 (8 oz.) carton of cool whip

Peach Topping:
  1 (3 oz.) package peach Jell-O
  1 ½ cups water
  ½ cup sugar
  2 T. cornstarch

  3 cups sliced Porter peaches (sprinkle with Fruit Fresh to prevent browning)

Cream together cream cheese, powdered sugar, and cool whip and place in graham cracker pie crust.

Mix together Jell-O, water, sugar, and cornstarch. Put in pan and cook until thick. Arrange peaches on top of cream layer and pour peach Jell-O topping over the peaches.

Refrigerate at least 3 hours before serving.

PEACH FACTS

🍑 One pound of fresh peaches will equal approximately:
- 3-4 medium sized peaches
- 2 cups sliced peaches
- 1 ½ cups of pulp or puree

🍑 It takes about two pounds of peaches to make one nine-inch pie.

🍑 A bushel of peaches should weigh in the neighborhood of 48 lbs. A half bushel should weigh around 23-24 lbs. A peck is a ¼ of a bushel and should weigh around 12 pounds. (To simplify our sales here at Livesay Orchards, we sell 8-qt boxes instead of pecks. The 8-qt box is just a peach or two shy of a peck.) To continue the math would mean that a half-peck basket of peaches is going to weigh around 5-6 lbs.

🍑 1 bushel of peaches makes anywhere from 18-24 quarts of canned peaches. (Depends on how many you eat when you are peeling them!)

🍑 There really is no way to know how many peaches are in a bushel of peaches. It all depends on the size of the peaches. Smaller peaches means there will be more peaches in a basket. Larger peaches mean the count will be lower.

🍑 One medium fresh peach has around 38 calories.

🍑 The peach is rich in vitamins A and C and iron.

🍑 Peaches are sodium free.

PEACH COBBLER

Nana Essary (Dear friend, neighbor, and employee)
2005 1ˢᵗ place winner at Porter Peach Festival

1 cup sugar
1 teaspoon cinnamon
½ teaspoon nutmeg
Oleo
¼ teaspoon almond extract
3 cups sliced fresh Porter peaches
2 crust pie dough

Mix sugar, cinnamon, and nutmeg together. Pour over peaches. Add almond extract. Pour peaches into bottom crust of deep dish pan. Dot with Oleo. Put top crust on and crimp edges. Sprinkle a little nutmeg and sugar on top. Cut slits in top for steam to escape. Put foil around crust edges and bake at 350 degrees for one hour or until brown.

Nana Essary, one of many of our valuable employees and friends, along with Prize peaches headed to the Festival.

PECAN PEACH COBBLER

Mandy Essary Stansberry (Nana's daughter and employee during high school)
2010 & 2011 1st Place Winner at Peach Festival

12 to 15 fresh Porter peaches, peeled and sliced
   (about 16 cups)
1/3 cup all-purpose flour
½ teaspoon ground nutmeg
3 cups sugar
2/3 cup butter
1 ½ teaspoons vanilla extract
Splash of almond extract
2 (15 oz.) packages refrigerated piecrusts
½ cup chopped pecans, toasted
5 tablespoons sugar, divided
Sweetened whipped cream

Preheat oven to 475°. Stir together peaches, flour, nutmeg, and 3 cups sugar in a Dutch oven. Bring to a boil over medium heat; reduce heat to low, and simmer 10 minutes. Remove from heat; stir in butter and vanilla. Spoon half of mixture into a lightly greased 13- x 9-inch baking dish.

Unroll 2 piecrusts. Sprinkle ¼ cup pecans and 2 tablespoons sugar over one piecrust; top with other piecrust. Roll to a 14- x 10-inch rectangle. Trim sides to fit baking dish. Place pastry over peach mixture in dish.

Bake at 475° for 20 to 25 minutes or until lightly browned. Unroll remaining 2 piecrusts. Sprinkle 2 tablespoons sugar and remaining ¼ cup pecans over one piecrust; top with remaining piecrust. Roll into a 12-inch circle. Cut into 1-inch strips, using a fluted pastry wheel. Spoon remaining peach mixture over baked pastry. Arrange pastry strings over peach mixture; sprinkle with remaining tablespoon sugar. Bake 15 to 18 minutes or until lightly browned. Serve warm or cold with whipped cream.

SUGAR SUBSTITUTE PEACH COBBLER
Dawna Livesay

4 cups peeled sliced peaches
2 cups Splenda
½ cup water
8 tablespoons butter
1 ½ cup self-rising flour
1 ½ cup milk
Ground cinnamon

Preheat oven to 350 degrees.

Combine peaches, 1 cup Splenda, and water in a sauce pan and mix well. Bring to boil and simmer for 10 minutes. Remove from heat.

Put butter in a 3-quart baking dish and place in oven to melt.

Mix remaining 1 cup Splenda, flour, and milk to prevent clumping. Pour mixture over melted butter. Do not stir. Spoon fruit on top, gently pouring in syrup. Sprinkle top with cinnamon. Batter will rise to top. Bake 45 to 55 minutes or until golden brown.

5 MINUTE PEACH MUG CAKE
Melanie Warren

1 tablespoon butter
3 tablespoons white cake mix
1 healthy pinch of cinnamon
1 not-so-healthy pinch of nutmeg
2 ½ tablespoons of milk
1 peach, peeled and diced

Place butter in a mug and melt in microwave. In a small bowl, whisk together cake mix and spices. Then stir in milk. Pour the mixture over the butter in the mug but don't stir. Layer peaches on top. Microwave for 2 to 3 minutes, until done. You'll just have to play around with your microwave and figure out how fast your microwave cooks. But that's okay; it just means you'll get to have peach cobbler a few nights in a row! Top with vanilla ice cream and a light dusting of cinnamon - the perfect ending to a long day!

Recipe Notes

My husband, Kent, has been a diabetic since he was a small child. Since we have to be careful with sweets, this cobbler recipe using Splenda instead of sugar allows Kent to enjoy fresh peach cobbler without compromising his health.

Dawna

HOMEADE PEACH ICE CREAM
Andrea Parnell

2 teaspoons vanilla
2 cups whipping cream
2 cans of peach pop
4 cups diced peeled peaches
1 – 2 cups of sugar
2 cans Eagle brand sweetened condensed milk

Mix first five ingredients well and pour in ice cream freezer can. Fill to the line with milk. Stir well and begin freezing.

Yield: 4 quarts

5 MINUTE PEACH FROZEN YOGURT
Melanie Warren

1 quart frozen peaches
¾ cup plain yogurt
1 tablespoon lemon juice
5 tablespoons honey

Put all ingredients in the bowl of the food processor and process for about 3 or 4 minutes, until very creamy. Add more honey for added sweetness. Eat immediately or you can store in an airtight container in the freezer for about a week. The sweetness of this dish comes from the honey; different honeys will give it a totally different flavor. My favorite honey to use in this recipe is from a local store in Jenks, Roark Acres Honey. It gives it an almost spicy taste that I love!

Yield: About 4 cups

PEACHES AND CREAM GELATIN
The Ledezma ladies (A family that we have been blessed to have work with us for almost 30 years)

5 oz. of peach flavored gelatin (D'Gari brand works well, which you can often find in the ethnic aisle but if not any gelatin will work)
15 oz. evaporated milk
3.5 oz. condensed milk
5 medium ripe peaches

Pour one liter of boiling water into a bowl and mix in gelatin mix until fully dissolved. Refrigerate. Cut the gelatin in cubes when it is completely set.

Use a blender to mix the evaporated and condensed milks. Chop the peaches. Mix gelatin, milk mixture, and peaches. Refrigerate for one hour and serve.

Yield: Around 6 one cup servings

PEACH BREAKFAST PARFAITS
Dawna Livesay

2 (6 oz.) cartons peach yogurt
½ cup granola
4 medium peaches, peeled, pitted, and coarsely chopped (about 3 cups)
Fresh berries, peach wedges

Divide half of the yogurt among 5 parfait glasses. Top with half of the granola. Divide chopped peaches among the glasses. Top with remaining yogurt and remaining granola. Serve immediately, or cover and chill up to 3 hours. Garnish with fresh berries and peach wedges, if you want to make it pretty!

Yield: 5 servings

PEACHY PIZZA
Dawna Livesay

Crust:
1 ½ cup all purpose flour
1 ½ sticks melted margarine
2 dashes of salt
½ to ¾ cup chopped pecans
1 tablespoon of sugar

Filling:
8 oz. cream cheese
8 oz. whipped topping
2 cups powdered sugar

Topping:
2 cups of chopped peaches
¾ cup sugar
2 tablespoons corn starch
1/3 cup water

Mix margarine, flour, salt, and sugar together. Stir in chopped pecans. Press into pizza pan and bake at 350 degrees for 10 to minutes until brown. Cream together cream cheese and sugar. Fold in whipped topping. Spread on cooled crust.

Place 2 cups of sliced peaches on top of filling.

Combine sugar, corn starch, and water and cook in sauce pan until thick. Spread on top of peaches.

CHICKEN WITH GRILLED PEACHES AND ARUGULA

Melanie Warren

4 6-oz. boneless chicken breasts
2 tablespoons plus 1 teaspoon olive oil
2 medium red onions, sliced into ½ inch rounds
3 peaches, wedged
1 bunch arugula, thick stems removed
3 tablespoons balsamic vinegar
3 oz. blue cheese crumbles
Salt and pepper

Heat grill to medium-high. Brush the chicken with 1 teaspoon of the olive and season with salt and pepper. In a bowl, toss the onions, peaches, 1 tablespoon of the oil, and ¼ teaspoon each salt and pepper.

Grill the chicken, onions, and peaches until the chicken is cooked through and the onions are tender, 6 to 7 minutes per side. The peaches will only need about 2 minutes per side to get nice charred marks, so remove those early.

Toss the arugula with the onions, peaches, vinegar, and remaining oil. Top with cheese.

Recipe Notes

Peaches and basil are AMAZING together! If chicken salad isn't your thing, try pan roasting some chicken breasts and peaches in olive oil and basil leaves—or add balsamic vinegar and honey—or add some onions and tomatoes. I'd give you a recipe, but I never do it the same way twice! Just have fun experimenting. You can't go wrong with these combinations.

Melanie

PEACH BASIL CHICKEN SALAD

Melanie Warren

Dressing:
1 peach, peeled and quartered
2 tablespoons lemon juice
1 tablespoon olive oil
½ tablespoon fresh basil
2 ½ tablespoon vinegar
½ teaspoon salt
½ teaspoon celery seed
2 teaspoons sugar
Pinch of white pepper
1/3 cup mayonnaise

Salad:
2 peaches, peeled and cubed
2 large chicken breasts, poached and shredded
3 ribs of celery, chopped
½ cup green onion, chopped
½ cup sweet bell peppers, chopped

Combine chicken with peaches, celery, onion, and pepper. Set aside. In a blender, combine all the dressing ingredients, blending until smooth. Pour over chicken mixture, stir to combine.

Cover and place in the refrigerator overnight to let the flavors meld together. I like to serve this recipe on toasted English muffins, but it would also be good on croissants or lettuce.

There's nothing prettier than a peach orchard in bloom. For about 10 days every spring, the peach trees put on a glorious show. However, when these beautiful blooms come before the last freeze of the season, a late cold snap can mean the end of that year's peach crop.

March 14, 1999 – A late snow storm made for some beautiful and unique pictures – but a very limited peach crop.

CROCKPOT PEACH BBQ BEEF
Dawna Livesay

1 beef roast
1 jar of Livesay Orchards' Porter Peach BBQ Sauce
½ package Lipton Onion Mushroom dry soup Mix
1 cup water
Hamburger buns (optional)

Place thawed roast beef in crockpot. Mix ½ package of the dry soup mix with 1 cup water and pour over roast. Cook 6 – 8 hours on low until fully done. Place roast on cutting board and shred by pulling apart with two forks or cut into bite-sized pieces. Place shredded roast into a non-stick skillet (or spray a skillet with non-stick cooking spray first) and stir in a jar of Livesay Orchard's Porter Peach BBQ Sauce on top of meat. Stir together well and heat over medium-low heat, stirring occasionally. Once the BBQ sauce is warm, the meat is ready to serve. Eat as is or on a bun.

This is a favorite in our household; there's usually no leftovers, which is good and bad because I don't have leftovers to serve the following night!

PEACH SALSA NACHOS
Dawna Livesay

1 lb of hamburger meat
1 jar Livesay Orchards' Porter Peach Salsa
1 bag of tortilla chips
Toppings:
    Livesay Orchards' fresh tomatoes
    Shredded lettuce
    Shredded cheese
    Chopped onion
    Sour cream
    More Peach Salsa

Brown and drain hamburger meat. Add Peach Salsa to skillet and stir to mix well. Heat over low heat. Serve over tortilla chips with toppings.

Recipe Notes

This is a variation of Granny's (Ramona Livesay) Salsa Nachos. She would crumble the chips then add the meat and toppings making it easy to eat with a fork. I prefer to pick up a chip and scoop up all the toppings onto it. This is a regular meal at our house, quick and easy and everyone likes it.

Dawna

PEACH GLAZED PORK CHOPS
Livesay Orchards

1 tablespoon olive oil
4 bone-in pork chops, ½ inch thick
2 teaspoons salt
1 teaspoon black pepper
1 teaspoon garlic powder
2 teaspoons paprika
1/3 cup Livesay Orchards Peach Jam
¼ cup Dijon mustard
2 teaspoons Worcestershire sauce
A few dashes of Tabasco sauce (optional)

Mix the jam, mustard, Worcestershire sauce, and hot sauce. Set the glaze aside.
In a separate bowl, combine the dry spices to make a rub.

Season each pork chop generously on both sides and rub the mixture into the meat.

Heat a skillet on medium high heat. Add the olive oil and the seasoned pork chops. Sear on each side for 2 minutes to get a nice crust. Once the pork chops are seared, pour the glaze over the pork chops and roast in a 400 degree oven until the pork chops are cooked through, about 4 – 8 minutes.

Let the pork chops rest for 5 minutes before serving. Then spoon some of the glaze from the pan over the top.

PORTER PEACH BBQ RIBS
Livesay Orchards

4 pounds ribs of your choice
2 teaspoons Worcestershire sauce
1 teaspoon vinegar
1 bottle Livesay Orchards Peach BBQ Sauce
2 tablespoons brown sugar
Salt and pepper

Rub the ribs with salt and pepper and place in slow cooker. Mix the rest of the ingredients together in a bowl and pour the sauce over the ribs, making sure everything is coated. Cover and cook on low for 6 to 8 hours, or until the ribs are tender. If you want, you can grill the ribs for a few minutes to caramelize the sauce right before serving. But it's not necessary – the ribs are finger-lickin' good with or without grilling.

Recipe Notes

While you are roasting your pork chops, roast some peaches to go along with your meal. For a savory side dish, half your peaches and remove the pit, sprinkle with salt and pepper and drizzle with a balsamic vinaigrette. Or, go for a sweet dessert. Top your halved peaches with a pat of butter and drizzle with honey. Then roast for 15 to 20 minutes. Top your savory roasted peaches with some blue cheese and your sweet peaches with some cream and cinnamon. Enjoy!

KAYLEE'S PEACH SALSA

Kaylee Herriman
Overall Champion at the 2012 Wagoner County 4-H Food Show

- 4 cups fresh Porter Peaches, diced
- 1 cup diced green bell peppers
- Juice of two limes
- 1 cup diced onions
- 1 small bunch of cilantro, chopped (about 1 cup)
- 1 – 3 finely chopped jalapeños (depends on how how you like it)
- Salt and black pepper to taste

Dice fresh peaches, mix in lime juice. Add bell pepper, onion, and cilantro. Toss well. Add jalapenos, salt, and pepper. Stir and refrigerate until chilled. Serve with your favorite tortilla chips.

GRILLED CHICKEN WITH PEACH SALSA

Livesay Orchards

- 4 boneless, skinless chicken breasts
- 5 tablespoons Southwestern Rub (see Farm Favorite Recipes)
- 1 jar Livesay Orchards Peach Salsa
  OR
  Make your own peach salsa!

Rub the Southwestern Rub mix on all sides of the chicken (it's best to let it sit for a bit if you can). Place chicken on a hot oiled grill. Grill chicken for 5 to 6 minutes per side, until done. Serve chicken hot with salsa.

GRILLED PEACHES AND GELATO

Melanie Warren

- 4 ripe peaches, halved and pitted
- ¼ cup salted butter
- Cinnamon sugar
- Cocoa powder
- Vanilla bean gelato

Melt the butter and brush it on the halved, pitted peaches. Grill over medium-low heat, covered, for 4 to 5 minutes on each side, until you develop those pretty char marks. Sprinkle with the cinnamon sugar or the cocoa powder and enjoy with vanilla bean gelato or ice cream.

Recipe Notes

Since most of us here on the farm spend our days outside in the summer selling peaches or picking watermelons, firing up the grill and cooking outside in the evenings isn't always high on our list. The good news is these grilling recipes can also be done inside on a grill pan or roasted in the oven.

We harvest peaches from early June to late September, generally. However, growing peaches is a full-year job. Peaches are a high maintenance and labor intensive crop to grow. Peach trees can produce around 25 – 30 years, but as they are a weak structured tree, Oklahoma winds, weather, and heavy fruit crops can shorten a tree's life. Maintaining healthy orchards requires some tender loving care to ensure that trees remain strong and producing for many years.

Caring for a peach crop begins in December or early January – dormant oil is applied to the trees to protect from insect damage.

From bud swell to harvest, trees are regularly sprayed to control damage to the trees or fruit from insects and disease.

Peach trees require heavy pruning every year. Pruning is done by hand in February.

In a good year, a peach tree will set on more fruit than it can bring to maturity . . .

"For everything there is a season, a time for every activity under heaven.

A time to be born and a time to die, a time to plant and a time to harvest."

Ecclesiastes 3:1,2, NLT

. . . so fruit must be thinned (see all the little green peaches under the trees) to allow for the tree to produce quality fruit.

Drip irrigation lines must be regularly checked and maintained to help combat dry Oklahoma summers.

Harvested peaches are graded and packaged to be sold to grocery stores or in our open air market.

Delicious Porter peaches on display, ready to go home with our loyal customers.

PEACH HINTS

- The best indicator that a peach is ripe is that the background color is yellow or cream. A blush or reddish color is not a sign of ripeness.

- A ripe peach will have a "peachy" aroma.

- The fresh ripe peach is firm but not hard.

- A ripe peach should be refrigerated immediately.

- Store fully ripe peaches in the refrigerator, spread out in one layer to minimize bruising. Fully ripe peaches will keep approximately 1 week.

- To allow peaches to ripen at room temperature, spread evenly on a counter, away from sunlight. In Oklahoma it is best not to leave them in any sort of bag or in a large bunch. If left in a closed container, our humid Oklahoma air will usually have some sort of mold spores that will thrive in a dark, closed area and you will be growing fuzz on your peaches that is not peach fuzz!

- When peaches are cut or peeled, keep their color bright by treating them with ascorbic acid (such as Fruit Fresh) or a citrus juice.

PEACH HINTS

- Firm peaches with a creamy or yellowish background will continue to ripen at room temperature. It could take anywhere from 1 day to 5 days. Be sure to check them each day and when they start to feel just a little bit soft, they should be placed in the refrigerator.

- Peaches that have the fuzz washed off need not be peeled. The skin is full of vitamins and minerals.

- Peaches are customarily classified in two general categories: Freestone and Clingstone. The clingstones are ones where the fruit does not separate from the pit. A freestone peach, *when fully ripe*, will usually pull away from the pit when you run a sharp knife all the way around the peach on the crease line; hold the peach between fingers of both hands; twist and pull apart gently. If a freestone peach is not fully ripe, it will not separate from the pit as easily as a fully ripe peach.

- Most peaches in the Livesay Orchard market are picked at a firm ripe stage. The firm ripe stage means that the peach will need anywhere from 2-5 days to continue ripening. This stage allows the peach to travel to your home with less bruising. If they were to be picked at full ripe stage, there would be a lot of bruising and loss of fruit on the trip to your home.

Pictured are: Apple Butter (pg 41), Apple Pie Poke Cake (pg 51), Crockpot Apple Cider (pg 45)

APPLE RECIPES

Good apple pies are a considerable part of our domestic happiness. — Jane Austen

APPLE BUTTER

Brenda Livesay

8-10 pounds of apples, or enough to make 16 cups of apple pulp
Water
1 cup cider vinegar
8 cups sugar
4 teaspoons cinnamon
½ teaspoon ground cloves
Canning jars and supplies

Wash and quarter the apples. Remove the stems and blossom end, but you may leave the core and seeds. There is a lot of naturally-occurring pectin in these areas that will help the butter set up later. Place the apples in large, heavy kettles with just a little bit of water in the bottoms. Cook the apples until tender. Be sure to stir often and use a low to medium heat so they won't scorch.

Press the apples through a sieve or food mill; measure your pulp and place in a heavy kettle. Cook over a low heat until the pulp is thick enough to round up on a spoon. Be sure to stir frequently while cooking to prevent scorching. Add sugar and spices and the cider vinegar. Cook slowly, stirring frequently, until thick. This usually takes another hour.

Pour into hot jars, leaving ¼ inch headspace. Adjust caps. Process the jars in a boiling-water bath for 10 minutes.

Yield: Around 6-7 pints

Recipe Notes

I like to use a mixture of apple varieties when making apple butter. Some of the best apple butter we made was after a high school science project. Our son was testing the sugar content of different varieties of apples. That meant we had bought 3—5 apples of each variety in several grocery stores. We only needed 1 slice from each apple so we cooked the rest and made apple butter. The flavor was fantastic!

Brenda

BLACKBERRY APPLE JELLY

Brenda Livesay

3 pounds blackberries (about 2 ½ quarts)
1 ¼ cups water
7 to 8 medium apples
Additional water
Bottled apple juice (optional) (This is a great way to use up any left-over Crockpot Apple Cider!)
¼ cup lemon juice
8 cups sugar
2 pouches (3 ounces each) liquid fruit pectin
You will also need a strainer and some cheesecloth or a jelly bag

In a large kettle, combine the blackberries and water; simmer for 5 minutes. Strain the berries through a jelly bag or a strainer lined with clean cheesecloth, reserving the juice and discarding the pulp.

Remove and discard the stem and blossom ends from the apples (do not pare or core); cut into small pieces. Place the apples in the kettle; add just enough water to cover. Simmer until the apples are soft, about 20 minutes. Strain the apples through the same jelly bag or strainer and cheesecloth, reserving the juice and discarding the pulp. Measure the reserved blackberry and apples juice. You will need 4 cups. If there is not enough juice to make 4 cups, add some bottled apple juice or water to make the needed 4 cups. Stir in lemon juice and sugar. Bring to a full rolling boil, stirring constantly. Add pectin, stirring until mixture boils. Boil for 1 minute. Remove from the heat; skim off foam. Pour hot into hot jars, leaving ¼ inch headspace. Adjust caps. Process for 15 minutes in a boiling-water bath.

Yield: About 9 half-pint jars

APPLE RAISIN BREAD

Brenda Livesay

2 packages (¼ ounce each) active dry yeast
1 ½ cups warm water, divided (110-115 degrees)
1 teaspoon sugar
3 eggs, beaten
1 cup applesauce
½ cup honey
½ cup vegetable oil
2 teaspoons salt
8 to 9 cups all-purpose flour
1 ½ cups diced peeled apples
2 tablespoons lemon juice
1 ½ cups raisins

Glaze:
    1 egg, beaten
    Sugar

In a small bowl, combine yeast, ½ cup warm a water, and sugar; set aside to let the yeast become active.

In a large bowl, combine eggs, applesauce, honey, oil, and remaining water; mix well. Stir in yeast mixture. Gradually add enough flour to form a soft dough. Knead on a floured surface until smooth and elastic, about 10 minutes. Place dough in a greased bowl, turning once to grease top. Cover and let rise in a warm place until doubled, about 1 hour. Punch down and turn over in bowl. Cover and let rise 30 more minutes.

In a small bowl, combine apples, lemon juice, and raisins. Divide dough into three parts; knead one third of the apple mixture into each part. Shape into round flat balls. Place each in a greased 8 inch round baking pan. Cover and let rise until doubled, about 1 hour. For glaze, brush each loaf with the beaten egg and sprinkle with sugar. Bake at 350 degrees for 30 to 35 minutes, or until bread sounds hollow when tapped.

Yield: 3 loaves

Teaching people about agriculture and how food is grown has always been an important part of our life. Here's Steve giving a tour to local school children in the early 1980s.

STREUSEL-TOPPED APPLE MUFFINS

Marsha Chasteen (Brenda's sister and long-ago peach seller)

2 1/3 cups all purpose flour
1 tablespoon baking powder
3/4 tsp ground cinnamon
1/2 tsp salt
1/8 tsp ground cloves
1 large egg
1/2 cup granulated sugar
1/4 cup vegetable oil
1/2 tsp vanilla
1 cup sweetened applesauce
2 cooking apples (peeled, cored and cut into 1/4 inch dice – about 2 cups)

Topping:
    1/4 cup butter at room temperature
    1/2 cup pecans chopped
    1/3 cup packed light brown sugar
    1/3 cup all purpose flour

Heat oven to 375°. Line 12 muffin tins with liners. In large bowl, mix flour, baking powder, cinnamon, salt, and cloves. In medium sized bowl, whisk egg, sugar, oil, and vanilla. Add applesauce. Make well in center of dry ingredients. Pour egg mixture into well; stir just until dry ingredients are moistened. Fold in diced apples. Divide among 12 muffin cups

In clean bowl, mix butter, nuts, sugar, and flour until crumbly. Sprinkle over tops of muffins. Bake at 375° for 22-25 minutes. Let cool in pan 5 minutes. Remove muffins to wire rack. Sprinkle with powdered sugar just before serving if desired.

In recent years, Dawna has worked hard at developing and expanding our school tours. Every fall, hundreds of elementary school children come to the farm to pick apples, pumpkins and learn about growing crops.

CROCKPOT APPLE CIDER

Melanie Warren

9 medium apples of assorted types
1 orange
3 cinnamon sticks
1 whole nutmeg
2 teaspoons whole cloves
½ teaspoon whole allspice
12 – 16 cups water
1/3 – 2/3 cup brown sugar (or other sweetener)

Wash apples and the orange and roughly cut into quarters. Don't worry about removing peels, seeds, or stems. Place fruit in crockpot along with the mulling spices. Cover with water, filling the crock-pot until it is nearly full. Cook on high heat for 3-4 hours, or on low heat for 6-8 hours.

About an hour before the apples are done cooking, when your apple and orange slices are soft, use a potato masher (or side of a big spoon or whatever utensil you have handy) to mash the fruit. Finish cooking for one more hour.

Use a fine mesh strainer or cheesecloth (or we discovered that disposable cheap coffee filters work well in the place of cheesecloth and then you can just throw them away) to press out the apple cider juice into a pitcher or pot. Sweeten to taste. I like to use brown but you could use white sugar or whatever type of sweetener you have.

Yield: About 3 liters

Recipe Notes

This recipe is a little on the time consuming side, but the taste is so much better than store-bought that once you taste it, you'll know the effort was worth it! If you are making a couple pots of this for a gathering or party, I would recommend cooking this up the day before. It re-heats well and will make the day of the party much less busy. As a added benefit, your house will smell like heaven when you cook up this cider!

Melanie

APPLES AND HOMEMADE SALTED CARAMEL SAUCE

Melanie Warren

3 cups granulated sugar, sifted (it won't work well if you have lumps!)
1 cup water
1 teaspoon vanilla extract
4 tablespoons salted butter
¾ cup heavy cream
1 teaspoon kosher salt
Apple slices for dipping

Optional:
    8 oz. block cream cheese
    Toffee bits

Spread sugar evenly in the bottom of a heavy duty large sauce pan. Pour in water and heat over medium heat. Do not stir. (Really, resist the urge and do not stir!) Bring to a boil. The sugar will begin to bubble and dissolve. If some of the sugar isn't dissolving, you can gently kind of swirl the pan around to help it dissolve.

Watch for the color to change from clear to a golden color. The caramel should begin to smoke a little and then will deepen to that reddish-brown caramel color. Once the mixture turns that reddish-brown color and you can start to smell the caramel, *immediately* remove from heat and stir in the vanilla, butter, cream, and salt. You will want to get these ingredients stirred in as quickly as possible, so make sure you have these items already out and measured. Stir with a heat-proof spoon or spatula until smooth.

Once cooled, you can serve alone with apple slices OR pour over a block of cream cheese and sprinkle with toffee bits. This recipe will store in the refrigerator for about a week. To rewarm saved caramel sauce, you can heat up slowly on the stovetop, stirring occasionally. You can also warm up in the microwave, cooking in little 7 – 8 second increments and stirring after each increment.

Yields: about 2 cups of sauce

Recipe Notes

I'll be honest. I botched this caramel recipe terribly the first one or two or ten times I made it. It's a test of patience at first, waiting for the sugar to caramelize, but then it's a race to the finish line! Just push through a few scorched pans of sugar and you'll get the hang of it. Trust me, it's worth the effort. This caramel sauce is rich and creamy and one of my favorite fall entertaining recipes.

Melanie

TAFFY APPLE SALAD
Marsha Chasteen

½ cup sugar
1 tablespoon flour
1 (8 oz.) can crushed pineapple in unsweet juice
1 egg
2 tablespoon vinegar
5-6 Granny Smith apples
   (can use 1 red Gala apple for color)
1 (8 oz.) carton Cool Whip, thawed
1 cup chopped roasted peanuts (optional)

Mix sugar and flour in medium saucepan. Add pineapple, egg, and vinegar. Mix well and cook over low heat until thick. Let cool and then refrigerate until cold. Core and dice apples (leave the skins on for color). Mix cold sauce and Cool Whip and add to apples in a large bowl. Mix in peanuts. Chill and serve.

DAWNA'S APPLE SALAD
Dawna Livesay

3 Livesay Orchards Fuji apples
3 Livesay Orchards Granny Smith apples
Fruit Fresh or 2 tablespoons lemon juice
1 cup chopped new crop pecans (usually
   harvested between October and December)
2 celery stalks, chopped
1 cup golden raisins (optional)
1 (8 oz.) container of Cool Whip
1 (6 oz.) container of plain yogurt

Core apples then cut them into bite-sized chunks. Sprinkle apples with Fruit Fresh or lemon juice to keep them from browning. Stir pecans, celery, and raisins with apples. Mix Cool Whip and yogurt together then add to apple mixture. Sprinkle a few chopped pecans on top (or a lot – we like new crop pecans!).

Recipe Notes
If it's early in the apple season at Livesay Orchards (August or September), I use Gala or Golden Delicious Apples for the sweet apples and Jonathan in place of the Granny Smith Apples.

Dawna

PORK CHOPS AND FRIED APPLES
Melanie Warren

2 tablespoons butter
4 pork chops (boneless or boned, your preference)
3 tablespoons brown sugar
1 teaspoon ground cinnamon
½ teaspoon ground nutmeg
¼ teaspoon salt
4 medium tart apples, thinly sliced (Granny Smith and Jonathan apples work great for this recipe)
2 tablespoons chopped pecans

In a large skillet, heat 1 tablespoon of the butter over medium heat. Add pork chops and cook 4-5 minutes on each side, until a thermometer reads 145 degrees. Meanwhile, in a small bowl, mix brown sugar, cinnamon, nutmeg, and salt.

Remove pork chops and keep warm. Add apples, pecans, brown sugar mixture, and remaining butter to pan. Cook and stir until apples are tender. Serve with chops.

FRIED APPLES
Kent Livesay

4 Livesay Orchards Jonathan apples
1 tablespoon butter
Dash of cinnamon (optional)

Core and slice apples, leaving the peel on. Place butter and apples in skillet. If available, cover skillet to speed cooking time. Heat until apples are soft. Sprinkle on cinnamon if desired.

If it's later in the season, Granny Smith apples are also delicious fried. They cook slower, but they keep their shape better than Jonathan apples.

Recipe Notes

Kent was a bachelor until age thirty-five when he married me. This was one of a few meals he cooked for himself and became very good at making this. He cooked sausage patties and canned biscuits to serve along with the fried apples. This is now one of my favorite meals. I prefer slicing my biscuit and adding the fried apples to it. I now cook the apples without the butter by spraying a non-stick pan with cooking spray.

Dawna

FRESH APPLE CAKE
Brenda Livesay

1 ¾ cup coarsely chopped peeled apples
1 cup sugar
1 1/3 cup flour
1 teaspoon baking soda
1 teaspoon cinnamon
½ teaspoon nutmeg
½ teaspoon ground allspice
½ cup vegetable oil
1 egg
½ cup raisins or dried cranberries
½ cup chopped pecans or walnuts

In a large mixing bowl combine the prepared apples and sugar; let stand for 10 minutes to allow the sugar to dissolve into the apples. Sift flour, soda, and spices and set aside. Blend oil and egg into apple-sugar mixture. Add dry ingredients, stirring just until blended (will be a very stiff mixture). Fold in raisins and nuts. Spread evenly in a greased 8-inch square pan. Bake at 350 degrees for 50-55 minutes. Cool at least 10 minutes. Sprinkle with powdered sugar.

APPLE NUT CAKE
Geraldine Dilbeck (long-time neighbor)

2 cups self-rising flour
2 cups sugar
1 cup cooking oil
2 eggs, beaten
1 teaspoon vanilla
2 cups chopped apples
1 cup chopped pecans or walnuts

Mix blended. (Will be a very stiff mixture) Fold in raisins and nuts. Spread evenly in a greased 8 inch square pan. Bake at 350 degrees for 50-55 minutes. Cool at least 10 minutes. Sprinkle with powdered sugar.

Yield: 6-8 servings

This Model A is the first tractor that CD and Maude Livesay bought new, back in 1947. It still runs today, though it is retired from farm work.

APPLE DANISH

Brenda Livesay

Pastry:
- 3 cups all-purpose flour
- ½ teaspoon salt
- 1 cup shortening
- 1 egg yolk
- ½ cup milk

Filling:
- 6 cups sliced peeled apples
- 1 ½ cups sugar
- ¼ cup butter or margarine, melted
- 2 tablespoons all-purpose flour
- 1 teaspoon ground cinnamon

Glaze:
- 1 egg white, lightly beaten
- ½ cup powdered sugar
- 2 to 3 teaspoons water

In a mixing bowl, combine flour and salt; cut in shortening until mixture resembles coarse crumbs. Combine egg yolk and milk; add to flour mixture. Stir just until dough clings together. Divide dough in half. On a lightly floured surface, roll half of dough into a 13 x 9 rectangle; transfer into a greased 13 x 9 inch baking pan. Set aside.

In a bowl, mix together the filling ingredients; spoon over pastry in pan. Roll out remaining dough and place over the filling. Brush the top pastry with the egg white. Bake at 375 degrees for 40 minutes or until golden brown. Cool on a wire rack.

Visitors always notice and talk about our "No Swearing!" sign. Kent and Steve's Grandma Rudisell, Madeline's mother, put these signs up (there used to be 2) in the early 1970s. According to them, no one dared use bad language on the farm, at least not when she was around!

APPLE PIE POKE CAKE

Melanie Warren

1 white cake (prepared in a 13×9 baking dish)
1 cup light brown sugar, packed
3 ½ cups diced fresh apples (any kind; I like a mixture of Fuji and Granny Smith)
¼ cup water
1 tsp cinnamon
¼ tsp nutmeg
¼ tsp salt
14 oz. can sweetened condensed milk
1 box (3.4 oz.) instant vanilla pudding mix
2 cups milk
1 tsp cinnamon
12 oz. whipped topping, thawed

Prepare white cake according to box directions for a 13×9 cake.

While cake is baking, work on cooking the apples. In a large skillet, whisk together the brown sugar with water, 1teaspoon cinnamon, nutmeg, and salt. Heat over medium high heat until bubbly, and then add diced apples. You can peel if you want, or leave the skins on. I leave the skins on because I don't like peeling and I kind of like the chewier texture. Reduce heat to low and simmer apples about 12-15 minutes.

When cake is done baking, poke holes all over (meat thermometers work well for this, but you can use a fork or skewer or whatever is in your utensil drawer). Pour can of sweetened condensed milk over hot cake. Then pour apple mixture. Spread and smooth until apples are evenly disbursed over top of cake and liquids have drained into the poked holes of the cake.

Refrigerate 3-4 hours or overnight.

While cake is in refrigerator, whisk the vanilla pudding with milk and 1 teaspoon cinnamon until smooth. Refrigerate until ready to serve.

When ready to serve cake, combine pudding mixture with thawed Cool Whip. Spread over cake, slice, and serve.

CHOCOLATE APPLE CAKE
Brenda Livesay

1 ½ cups flour
½ cup unsweetened cocoa powder
1 ½ teaspoons baking powder
½ teaspoon baking soda
½ teaspoon salt
½ cup (1 stick) butter, melted
½ cup buttermilk
1 ¼ cups sugar
2 large eggs
1 tablespoon vanilla
½ cup semi-sweet chocolate chips
2 cups coarsely chopped tart apples
Powdered sugar

Sift flour, cocoa, baking powder, baking soda, and salt into a large bowl. In a medium bowl, whisk butter, buttermilk, and sugar until smooth. Blend in eggs and vanilla. Pour the liquid mixture over the dry ingredients and mix with rubber spatula until thoroughly combined. Stir in chocolate chips and apples and spoon into a greased 8 inch square baking dish. Bake for 50 minutes, or until done in the center, in a 350 degree oven. Cool completely on a wire rack and dust with powdered sugar before serving.

APPLE FRITTERS
Marsha Chasteen

1 beaten egg
1 cup milk
1 cup chopped apple
¼ cup sugar
¼ tsp salt
1 tsp grated orange peel
3 Tbsp orange juice
½ tsp vanilla
2 cups flour
1 Tbsp baking powder
Vegetable oil for frying
Sifted powdered sugar

In mixing bowl combine beaten egg, milk, chopped apple, sugar, salt, orange peel, juice, and vanilla. Stir together flour and baking powder in a separate bowl. Fold into egg mixture, stirring just until all flour is moistened. Drop batter by rounded teaspoon into hot oil (350°). Fry until deep golden brown, about 3-4 minutes, turning once. Drain fritters thoroughly on paper towel. Roll in sugar or sift over tops.

EASY APPLE DUMPLINGS
Melanie Warren

2 cans of crescent rolls
3 - 4 tart apples
1 ½ cups sugar
½ cup butter
1 teaspoon cinnamon
1 (12 oz.) can lemon-lime pop

Spray a 13x9 baking dish or pan with non-stick spray. Peel and slice apples into 16 pieces. Roll each apple slice in 1 section of crescent roll. Place in baking dish. Melt butter; add sugar and cinnamon and pour over apples. Pour can of lemon-lime pop over all. Bake at 350 degrees for 45 minutes. Serve warm with vanilla ice cream.

Yield: 16 dumplings

ENGLISH APPLE PIE
Brenda Livesay

3 - 5 apples, peeled and sliced
½ cup sugar
½ teaspoon cinnamon
1 cup brown sugar
¼ cup butter
1 cup flour

Spray a 1 ½ qt casserole dish with non-stick spray and fill about ¾ of the way with sliced apples. On top of the apples, sprinkle sugar and cinnamon.

In a bowl, mix brown sugar and butter until smooth. Then add flour. Press the flour mixture on top of apples. Bake at 350 degrees for 40 minutes.

Serve warm with vanilla ice cream.

Apple picking in the 1970s

HONEYED APPLE TREAT

Dawna Livesay

4 tart apples, cored and sliced (Jonathan or Granny Smith are great)
2 cups granola with fruit and nuts
¼ cup honey
2 tablespoons butter, melted
1 teaspoon cinnamon
½ teaspoon nutmeg
Garnishes: whipped topping, additional nutmeg

Combine apples and granola in a slow cooker. In a separate bowl, combine honey, butter, cinnamon, and nutmeg; pour over apple mixture and mix well. Cover and cook on low setting for 8 hours. Garnish servings with a dollop of whipped topping and sprinkle with additional nutmeg.

Yields: 4 – 6 servings

Pictured are: Pumpkin Bread (pg 58), Pumpkin Dip (pg 62), Chocolate Pumpkin Snickerdoodles (pg 61)

PUMPKIN RECIPES

I'm so glad I live in a world where there are Octobers. – L.M. Montgomery

PUMPKIN CHOCOLATE CHIP MUFFINS
Brenda Livesay

4 eggs
2 cups sugar (sometimes I substitute 1 cup sugar and 1 cup Splenda)
1 can of pumpkin (15-16 ounces)
1 ½ cups vegetable oil
3 cups all-purpose flour
2 teaspoons baking soda
2 teaspoons baking powder
1 teaspoon ground cinnamon
1 teaspoon salt
2 cups semisweet chocolate chips (I like to use the miniature chips, but the regular ones work well also)

In a large mixing bowl, beat eggs, sugar, pumpkin, and oil until smooth. Combine flour, baking soda, baking powder, cinnamon, and salt; add to pumpkin mixture and mix well. Fold in chocolate chips. Fill paper-lined muffin cups three-fourths full. Bake at 400 degrees for 16-20 minutes or until muffins test done. Cool in pan for 10 minutes before removing to wire rack.

Yield: about 24 standard-size muffins

Recipe Notes

These Pumpkin Chocolate Chip Muffins are always a big hit at school and church events, and now, Melanie gets requests to take them to work in Tulsa. Just remember, this is a quick bread so be sure to mix by hand and not an electric mixer so that your muffins won't be tough!

Brenda

MAPLE PUMPKIN MUFFINS
Marsha Chasteen

2 cups all-purpose flour
¾ cup plus 2 tablespoons packed brown sugar
2 tsp baking powder
1 tsp ground cinnamon
½ tsp baking soda
½ tsp pumpkin pie spice
¼ tsp salt
2 eggs
1 cup canned pumpkin
¾ cup evaporated milk
¼ cup vegetable oil
3 tablespoon maple syrup, divided
½ cup chopped pecans or walnuts
3 oz. cream cheese, softened

Topping:
 ¼ cup chopped pecans or walnuts
 2 tsp brown sugar

In a large bowl, combine flour, ¾ cup brown sugar, baking powder, cinnamon, baking soda, pumpkin pie spice, and salt. In medium sized bowl, whisk the eggs, pumpkin, milk, oil, and 1 tablespoon syrup; stir into dry ingredients just until moistened. Fold in nuts.

In a small mixing bowl, beat cream cheese and remaining brown sugar and syrup until smooth. Gently stir into batter until mixture appears swirled.

Fill greased or paper-lined muffin cups about three-fourths full. Combine topping ingredients; sprinkle over batter. Bake at 400° for 20-25 minutes or until a toothpick comes out clean. Cool for 5 minutes before removing from the pan to a wire rack.

Yield: 1 dozen

CRANBERRY PUMPKIN BREAD

Brenda Livesay

3 cups all-purpose flour
1 teaspoon salt
1 teaspoon baking soda
1 teaspoon baking powder
1 teaspoon ground cinnamon
½ teaspoon ground ginger
½ teaspoon nutmeg
½ teaspoon cloves
3 eggs
2 cups canned pumpkin
1 cup canola oil (or your choice of cooking oil)
2/3 cup sugar
2/3 cup packed brown sugar
1 Tablespoon vanilla
1 ½ cups dried cranberries
1 cup chopped nuts

In a large bowl, combine the flour, salt, baking soda, baking powder, and spices. In another bowl, combine the eggs, pumpkin, oil, sugars, and vanilla; stir into dry ingredients just until moistened. Fold in cranberries and pecans.

Pour into 2 greased loaf pans. Bake at 350 degrees for 50-55 minutes or until a toothpick inserted near the center comes out clean. Cool for 10 minutes before removing from pans to wire racks.

Yield: 2 loaves

PUMPKIN BREAD

Brenda Livesay

1 cup packed brown sugar
½ cup sugar
1 cup cooked or canned pumpkin
½ cup vegetable oil
2 eggs
2 cups sifted all-purpose flour
1 teaspoon soda
½ teaspoon each salt, nutmeg and cinnamon
¼ teaspoon ginger
1 cup raisins
½ cup chopped nuts
¼ cup water

Combine sugars, pumpkin, oil, and eggs; beat until well blended. Sift together flour, soda, salt, and spices; add to pumpkin mixture and mix well by hand. Stir in raisins, nuts, and water. Spoon batter into a well-oiled loaf pan. Bake at 350 degrees for 65 to 75 minutes or until done when tested. Let cool for about 10 minutes and then turn out on a rack to cool.

Yield: 1 loaf

Recipe Notes

Both of these recipes could also be made into muffins. Just line a muffin tin with paper liners and bake for 15—20 minutes or until done.

When making the pumpkin bread, I like to double the recipe and make two loaves so I use up the whole can of pumpkin. This bread also freezes well.

Brenda

PUMPKIN CINNAMON ROLLS

Melanie Warren

Dough:
- ¼ oz. package yeast
- ½ cup warm water
- ½ cup scalded milk
- ¼ cup sugar
- 1/3 cup butter, melted
- 1 teaspoon salt
- 1 cup canned pumpkin puree
- ½ teaspoon pumpkin pie spice
- ¼ teaspoon ground nutmeg
- ¼ teaspoon ground clove
- 1 egg
- 4 – 5 cups all-purpose flour

Filling:
- ½ cup softened butter, plus more for pan
- ¾ cup sugar, plus more for pan
- ¼ cup brown sugar
- 2 tablespoons cinnamon
- 1 teaspoon pumpkin pie spice

Maple Cream Cheese Icing:
- 4 oz. cream cheese, softened
- ¼ cup unsalted butter, softened
- 1 ½ cups powdered sugar
- ½ teaspoon vanilla extract
- ½ teaspoon maple extract
- ¼ teaspoon salt

In a small bowl, dissolve yeast in warm water and set aside. Combine milk, sugar, melted butter, pumpkin, spices, salt, and egg. Mix in two cups of flour and mix with electric mixer until smooth. Add yeast mixture. Mix in remaining flour until dough is easy to handle. Knead dough on a lightly floured surface for 5 to 10 minutes. Place in a well-greased bowl, cover, and let rise until doubled in size, usually about 1 ½ hours.

When doubled in size, punch down dough. Roll out on floured surface into a 15 by 9 inch rectangle. Spread softened butter all over dough. In a small bowl, mix together sugar, cinnamon, and pumpkin pie spice. Then sprinkle over buttered dough. Beginning on the long side, roll up dough and pinch the edges together to seal it. Cut into 12 to 15 slices, depending on how big you like your rolls.

Coat the bottom of a 13 x 9 inch baking pan with butter and sprinkle with sugar. Place cinnamon roll slices close together in the pan and let rise until dough is doubled, about 45 minutes. Bake for about 45 minutes in a 350 degree oven.

While baking, mix cream cheese, butter, powdered sugar, salt, vanilla, and maple extract until smooth. Add more powdered sugar if needed to make thicker. Spread over slightly cooled rolls.

Fall 2009, from left to right:

Brenda and Steve Livesay and their children Melanie and Brian, Kent and Dawna Livesay and their children, Kyle and Nathan, Ramona and David Livesay

Known as Papa and Granny to the grandkids, David and Ramona Livesay played an active role in the day to day operations of the farm far after they reached "retirement age". Granny worked in the market, kept paperwork straight and handled a lot of the communication with grocery stores while Papa David delivered produce to stores, made hundreds of part runs and lots of other "behind the scenes" jobs that kept the farm running smooth.

PUMPKIN COOKIES
Brenda Livesay

2 cups packed brown sugar
2 cups pumpkin
1 cup vegetable oil
2 teaspoons vanilla
4 cups flour
2 teaspoons baking soda
2 teaspoons baking powder
1 teaspoon salt
1 teaspoon cinnamon
1 teaspoon nutmeg
½ teaspoon ginger
2 cups raisins
1 cup chopped nuts

Beat together sugar, pumpkin, oil, and vanilla. Sift together dry ingredients; add dry ingredients to pumpkin mixture and stir until smooth. Fold in raisins and nuts. Drop by spoonfuls onto greased baking sheets. Bake at 350 degrees for 12-15 minutes.

Yield: 6 to 8 dozen

Recipe Notes

Both of these cookies are very moist and cake-like. They won't spread out like normal cookies do in the oven. They also will look very soft and maybe underbaked after baking the recommended time, but if you leave them in the oven longer they will dry out quickly.

Brenda & Melanie

CHOCOLATE PUMPKIN SNICKERDOODLES
Melanie Warren

½ cup unsalted butter
¼ cup packed brown sugar
1 cup granulated sugar, divided
1 teaspoon vanilla extract
6 tablespoons pumpkin puree
1 ½ cups flour
¼ teaspoon salt
¼ teaspoon baking powder
¼ teaspoon baking soda
2 teaspoons ground cinnamon, divided
1 teaspoon pumpkin pie spice
½ cup white chocolate chips

Melt the butter in the microwave. In a medium bowl, whisk the melted butter, brown sugar, and ½ cup granulated sugar together until you've worked out all the brown sugar lumps. Whisk in the vanilla and pumpkin until smooth. Set aside.

In a large bowl, mix together the flour, salt, baking powder, baking soda, 1 ½ teaspoons cinnamon, and pumpkin pie spice. Pour the wet ingredients into the dry ingredients and mix together. Fold in white chocolate chips. Cover the dough and chill for 30 minutes or up to 3 days.

Roll the dough into balls, using a heaping tablespoon full for each ball. Mix together the remaining ½ cup of sugar and ½ teaspoon of cinnamon. Roll the balls generously in the cinnamon sugar mixture and arrange on baking sheets. Slightly flatten the dough balls.

Bake the cookies for 8 – 10 minutes. Cool for at least 10 minutes on cookie sheet before transferring to a wire rack to finish cooling.

Yields: 18 cookies

PUMPKIN DIP

Jenna Dupree (3rd generation employee and neighbor)

1 (8 oz.) package cream cheese, softened
2 cups powdered sugar
2 teaspoon cinnamon
½ teaspoon ginger
1 (15 oz.) can pumpkin

Use a mixer to cream together cream cheese and powdered sugar. Mix spices in well. Mix in pumpkin until the dip is very creamy. Refrigerate and serve.

> **Recipe Notes**
>
> Jenna said that if you have a stand mixer, you can use the whipping attachment to make the dip super creamy.
>
> I made this dip for Thanksgiving this year and everyone loved it! I served it with gingersnap cookies and graham crackers and by accident also picked up some cinnamon graham crackers, which actually ended up being my favorite!
>
> — Melanie

PUMPKIN & CHOCOLATE CHIP OAT BARS

Melanie Warren

3 cups oats
2 teaspoons baking powder
½ teaspoon salt
1 ¼ teaspoon cinnamon
¼ teaspoon pumpkin pie spice
1 cup canned pumpkin puree
2 teaspoons vanilla extract
½ cup unsweetened applesauce
½ cup brown sugar
1 tablespoon olive oil
1/3 cup chocolate chips (I prefer mini chips)

Mix together oats, baking powder, baking soda, salt, and spices. Set aside. In a separate large bowl, whisk together pumpkin, brown sugar, vanilla extract, oil, and applesauce until smooth and creamy. Slowly add in the oat mixture and mix until just combined.

Gently fold in chocolate chips. Pour batter into a 9x11 inch pan that has been greased. (I like to sprinkle a few more chips on the top). Bake for 15 – 20 minutes in a 350 degree oven until a knife inserted into the center comes out clean.

PUMPKIN AND PECAN CHEESECAKE

Melanie Warren

Cheesecake:
- 2 cups graham cracker crumbs
- 1/3 cup finely chopped pecans
- 5 tablespoons butter, melted
- 3 tablespoons light brown sugar
- 4 (8 oz.) packages cream cheese, softened
- 1 cup granulated sugar
- 1 teaspoon vanilla extract
- 4 large eggs
- 1 1/2 cups canned pumpkin
- 1 1/2 tablespoons lemon juice

Topping:
- 1 cup packed brown sugar
- 1/3 cup whipping cream
- ¼ cup butter
- 1 cup powdered sugar, sifted
- 1 teaspoon vanilla extract

Glazed Pecans:
- 2 cups pecan halves
- ½ cup packed brown sugar
- 6 tablespoons dark corn syrup

Stir together first 4 ingredients in a bowl until well blended. Press mixture on bottom and 1½ inches up sides of a 9-inch springform pan. Bake 8 to 10 minutes or until lightly browned. Beat cream cheese, sugar, and vanilla on medium speed until blended and smooth. Add eggs, 1 at a time, beating just until blended after each addition. Add pumpkin and lemon juice, beating until blended. Pour batter into prepared crust. (Pan will be very full.)

Bake at 325° for 1 hour to 1 hour and 10 minutes or until almost set. Turn oven off. Let cheesecake stand in oven, with door closed, 15 minutes. Remove cheesecake from oven, and gently run a knife around outer edge of cheesecake to loosen from sides of pan. (Do not remove sides of pan.) Cool completely on a wire rack (about 1 hour). Cover and chill 8 to 24 hours.

Remove sides and bottom of pan, and transfer cheesecake to a serving plate. Bring brown sugar, whipping cream, and butter to a boil in a small saucepan over medium heat, stirring often. Boil, stirring occasionally, 1 minute; remove from heat. Gradually whisk in powdered sugar and vanilla until smooth. Let stand 5 minutes, whisking occasionally. Immediately pour slowly over top of cheesecake, spreading to within ¼ inch of edge. Stir together pecans, sugar, and corn syrup. Spread mixture into a lightly greased aluminum foil lined cake pan. Bake at 350 degrees for 10 – 13 minutes, stirring every few minutes. Spread in a single layer on wax paper to cool, separating pecans as they cool. When fully cooled, garnish cheesecake.

Recipe Notes

I got this recipe from Southern Living several years ago and it has become my customary dish to bring to Thanksgiving dinner. When garnishing, I usually just put a few pecans on top so it's easier to cut and then pass the rest around to let people garnish their individual pieces.

Melanie

Kent and David at the shed in the early 2000s

Steve and David at the shed in the mid-2000s

Steve with Madeline, Kent and Steve's mother, in 1976

Pictured are: Cheeseburger Cups (pg 74), Macaroni Salad (pg 71), Peanut Butter Squares (pg 80)

FARM FRIENDLY RECIPES

Farming can be a hectic lifestyle. Meals need to be simple and fast, easy to take to the field when the guys can't come to the house and easy to be reheated because farmers never get home for dinner at the time they tell their wives. These recipes are our favorite go-to meals here on the farm!

5 DAY SWEET PICKLES

Mildred Keel (Brenda's mother)

2 gallons cucumbers
3 tablespoons powdered alum
6 lbs white sugar
white vinegar
cold water
2 tablespoons whole allspice

Brine:
1 cup salt to ½ gallon water

Cover cucumbers with cold water brine. Let stand 2 days. Drain and cover with equal parts water and vinegar. Let stand for 2 days. Drain and cover with cold water and 3 tablespoons powdered alum. Let stand for 1 day and drain.

Mix together equal parts vinegar and water in a large pot. Add 6 cups sugar and 2 tablespoons whole allspice. Put cucumbers in and simmer for 2 hours over low heat.

Put in jars and seal with 1 or 2 cloves of garlic in each jar.

Recipe Notes

My grandmother, Mildred Keel, taught me how to make these pickles. I can't remember a time that Grammy didn't have a jar of these in the fridge and on the Sunday dinner table, always served in her green glass "pickle dish". When I was in college, I found an identical dish at a flea market for $7.95. Grammy later told me they must have seen a sucker coming when I walked in the door as she just paid a dime for her dish back in the 50s. I think that $7.95 was well spent though, and always serve pickles in my very own "pickle dish".

Melanie

FAVORITE FRUIT PUNCH
Brenda Livesay

4 ½ cups sugar (you can substitute Splenda for part of the amount)
8 cups water
1 large 46 oz. can canned pineapple juice
1 large 12 oz. can frozen lemonade concentrate
1 large 12 oz. can frozen orange juice concentrate
4 more cups water
1 or 2 quarts of 7-UP or ginger ale (depending on your preference)

This recipe makes 2 gallons. If you do not have a container that large, divide between two gallon containers. Dissolve sugar in the 8 cups water. Add pineapple juice, lemonade, orange juice, and the rest of the water. Just before serving add 7-UP or ginger ale. This recipe can definitely be made the day ahead of time; you just want to add the fizzy stuff right before serving. If you are going to be using an ice ring in a punch bowl, you may want to cut down on the water amounts just a little.

CANTALOUPE FRESCA
The Ledezma Ladies

1 cantaloupe
1 gallon water
2 cups sugar

Cut the cantaloupe in half and seed it. Scrape the cantaloupe meat into a large bowl or jar. Add the water and sugar and mix well until all the sugar is dissolved. Refrigerate for a couple of hours before serving.

Recipe Notes

We have served this punch at many a wedding, reception and wedding/baby shower and always receive lots of compliments.

Brenda & Melanie

We have a long tradition of growing watermelons in the Livesay family. To the left are pictures of C.D. Livesay (top) and his son, David, picking watermelons from their farm in Tuskegee, Oklahoma in the 1940s; Kent and Steve loading up a trailer of watermelons from Porter in the 1970s, and Brian Livesay picking watermelons around 2010.

One year, in 1974, a bad freeze hit late and completely wiped out the peach crop. Kent and Steve remember their parents decided to plant over 50 acres of watermelons that year to help compensate for the loss of the peach income. In Steve's words, "I thought that summer picking watermelons would never end!" 1996 was another year that the peaches completely froze out and we planted extra watermelons. It seemed like every square inch of the market that year was covered in watermelon bins!!

Picking watermelons is hard, back-breaking work. These days Steve and Brian are the principal watermelon pickers, while Brenda drives the tractor for them in the field.

SPICY GRILLED MELONS
Melanie Warren

¼ cup honey
¼ cup lime juice
2 teaspoons cayenne pepper
1 teaspoon salt (I like to use coarser sea salt)
½ cup mint, chiffonade
Watermelon
Cantaloupe

Cut the watermelon and cantaloupe into half-inch thick slices. Whisk together the honey, lime juice, cayenne pepper (can also use chili powder), and salt in a bowl. Brush the honey mixture over each side of the fruit pieces. Grill over a preheated grill for 2 to 3 minutes on each side. Serve with mint (and if you want, fresh cream).

SOUTHWEST GRILLED CHICKEN
Melanie Warren

1 teaspoon salt
2 teaspoons garlic powder
2 teaspoons chili powder
2 teaspoons ground cumin
2 teaspoons pepper
½ teaspoon cocoa powder
¼ cup olive oil
6 chicken breasts

Mix together seasonings and oil. Pour into a large resealable bag and add chicken breasts. Swoosh around until the chicken is well coated with the marinade mixture. Refrigerate for about 30 minutes. Remove chicken and discard the excess marinade. Grill on a preheated grill for about 5 – 7 minutes per side, turning frequently.

WATERMELON SWEET AND SPICY SALSA
Melanie Warren

3 cups chopped, seeded watermelon
½ cup chopped green bell pepper
2 tablespoons lime juice
4 tablespoons chopped fresh cilantro
1 tablespoon chopped green onion
2 tablespoons chopped jalapeno
½ teaspoon garlic salt

Combine all ingredients in a large bowl. Mix well and serve.

Recipe Notes

- This salsa is great with chips AND with grilled chicken, like this Southwestern Chicken.
- This Southwestern Chicken Rub is a staple in my kitchen. I make up a big batch or two every summer and use it for dry rubs and marinades.

Melanie

MARINATED TOMATO SALAD
Melanie Warren

5 – 6 medium fresh tomatoes, sliced
¼ lb fresh mushrooms, sliced
¾ cup vegetable oil
¼ cup red wine vinegar
3 garlic gloves, minced
1 tablespoon minced fresh parsley
½ teaspoon salt

In a large shallow dish, layer the tomatoes and mushrooms. In a bowl, whisk oil, vinegar, garlic, parsley, and salt. Pour over tomatoes and mushrooms. Cover and refrigerate for at least 4 hours, turning a couple of times.

MACARONI SALAD
Brenda Livesay

3 quarts of water
1 Tablespoon salt
2 cups elbow macaroni
½ cup Italian oil dressing
1 ½ cup sliced celery
½ cup grated carrots
½ cup chopped green onions
1 ½ cup diced cheddar cheese
1 cup diced ham
1 cup sour cream

Bring the water to boil in a large pot with the salt. Gradually add the macaroni and simmer until tender, stirring occasionally. Drain water from the macaroni and rinse with cold water; drain well. Place macaroni in a large bowl and stir in the Italian oil dressing. Cover bowl and place in refrigerator to marinate for at least 3 hours.

Combine the rest of the ingredients with the macaroni. Enjoy!

BAKED SQUASH
Melanie Warren

1/8 cup honey
4 tablespoons butter, melted
½ teaspoon salt
¼ teaspoon ground cinnamon
¼ teaspoon ground ginger
2 medium acorn squash

Mix the first five ingredients in a bowl. Cut the squash in half; remove and discard seeds. Fill squash halves with the butter mixture. Place in a greased baking dish. Cover with foil and cook for 1 hour in a 375 degree oven. Uncover and cook for another 10 minutes or so, until the mixture is bubbly.

BAKED SUMMER SQUASH WITH CHEESE
Marsha Chasteen

4 cups fresh yellow squash
16 saltine crackers crushed
1 cup shredded cheddar cheese
¼ cup onion chopped
1/2 cup canned evaporated milk
½ teaspoon salt
Black pepper to taste

Preheat oven to 350 degrees.

Cook sliced squash in microwave with ¼ cup water until tender. Spray a 9 inch square baking dish with non-stick cooking spray. Use half the precooked squash and place over the bottom of the dish. Add a layer of onion and half the shredded cheese. Add the remaining squash and another layer of cheese. In small bowl mix together milk, salt, and black pepper. Pour this mixture over the casserole. Add cracker crumbs on top and bake at 350 degrees for 20-25 min.

NO-KNEAD REFRIGERATOR ROLLS

Brenda Livesay

¾ cup boiling water
½ cup sugar
1 tablespoon salt
3 tablespoons shortening
1 cup warm water
2 packages of dry yeast
5 cups flour (all purpose or bread flour)
1 cup whole wheat flour
1 egg

In a large mixing bowl, mix the boiling water, sugar, salt, and shortening. Stir a little until the shortening starts to melt and let sit while measuring the rest of the ingredients.

In a smaller bowl, dissolve the yeast in the warm water and let set for about 5 minutes. Mix 1 cup of flour and the 1 cup of whole wheat flour together and add to the water/shortening mixture. Beat until very smooth. Add egg and dissolved yeast. Beat until well blended. Stir in remaining flour one cup at a time.

Place dough in greased bowl that has a sealable lid; brush top with some soft shortening. Store in refrigerator until doubled.

When ready to make rolls, punch the dough down and using greased hands, form the dough into desired shapes and place in greased muffin tins or pans. Lightly grease the tops of the rolls and cover and let them rise until doubled.

Bake at 400 degrees for 15-20 minutes.

Recipe Notes

- I usually make the dough the night before and let it set until morning. It will take 3—4 hours for the rolls to rise depending on how warm the room is.
- You can also use all-purpose flour for the entire amount of flour. Our family just likes the taste with a little whole wheat flour in it.
- This dough will keep in the refrigerator for 3—5 days.

Brenda

SPANISH RICE
Brenda Livesay

2-3 slices of chopped, cooked bacon
1 cup uncooked long grain rice
1 small can tomato sauce (8 oz.)
1 10 oz. can diced tomatoes with green chilies (I usually use mild flavored Rotel, but use your family's preference here)
1 cup water
1 tablespoon Worcestershire sauce
1 tablespoon brown sugar
¾ cup frozen corn (optional)

In a fairly large, heavy pan (this will need a tight fitting lid for later in the recipe), cook the 2-3 slices of bacon until well done, stir often while browning. When bacon is done, add the rest of the ingredients to the pan and stir well. Bring the mixture to boil with the lid off. Then, reduce the heat to low, put the lid on the pan and cook for 20 minutes. After 20 minutes, remove from heat and let set for 5-10 minutes before serving.

BROCCOLI RICE CASSEROLE
Mildred Keel

1 small onion, chopped
3 tablespoons margarine
1 can cream of chicken soup
2 – 3 cups of chopped broccoli, frozen and thawed OR fresh florets
½ cup milk
½ lb. Velveeta cheese
3 cups cooked rice
Grated cheddar cheese

Cook rice (to get 3 cups of cooked rice, cook a cup of rice with 2 cups of water). Bring water and rice to boil, reduce heat, cover with lid, and let simmer for about 20 minutes.

Sauté onion in margarine. Add chicken soup, milk, and Velveeta cheese. Heat until cheese melts smooth. Cook broccoli in another pan until it just begins to get tender.

Gently fold rice and broccoli into cheese mixture. Pour into a greased casserole dish and top with grated cheese (we like lots of cheese). Bake in 350 degree oven for 20 to 30 minutes or can be microwaved for 3 to 4 minutes until warmed throughout.

CHEESEBURGER CUPS
Brenda Livesay

1 lb. ground beef
½ cup ketchup
2 tablespoons brown sugar
1 tablespoon prepared mustard (our family likes the brown mustard in this recipe)
1 ½ teaspoons Worcestershire sauce
1 (12 oz.) tube of refrigerated buttermilk biscuits (I like to get the ones that are listed as flaky layers and the grand size)
½ cup cubed process cheese (Velveeta)

In a large skillet, cook beef over medium heat until no longer pink; drain. Stir in the ketchup, brown sugar, mustard, and Worcestershire sauce. Remove from heat; set aside.

Press a biscuit layer onto the bottom and up the sides of a greased muffin cup. Spoon beef mixture into cups; top with cheese cubes. Bake at 400 degrees for 14-16 minutes or until golden brown.

Yield: 4 servings

HASHBROWN CASSEROLE
Melanie Warren

5 eggs
1 (5 oz.) can evaporated milk
1 teaspoon salt
5 ½ cups frozen shredded hash brown potatoes, thawed
1 cup shredded cheddar cheese
¼ cup chopped onion
1 small jar (2 oz.) diced pimentos
1 cup of cooked, crumbled bacon and/or ham

Cook or prepare meat for casserole. In a large bowl, combine the eggs, milk, and salt and mix well. Stir in potatoes, cheese, onion, pimentos, and meat. Pour in an 8 inch square pan that has been well greased. Bake, uncovered, at 350 degrees for 45 – 50 minutes, or until a knife inserted near the center comes out clean.

Recipe Notes

These are really handy when having to take a meal to the field for the crew to eat a meal.

If you have time to make a big batch, the leftovers keep well in the fridge to warm up the next day for a quick lunch.

Brenda

CROCKPOT PIZZA

Brenda Livesay

1 package (12 ounces) wide egg noodles
1 ½ pounds ground beef
¼ cup chopped onion
1 jar (28 ounces) spaghetti sauce
1 ½ teaspoon Italian seasoning
1 package (3 ½ ounces) sliced pepperoni, cut into small pieces
1 small can (2.5 ounces) sliced olives, optional
3 cups shredded Italian blended cheeses
3 cups shredded cheddar cheese

Cook noodles according to package directions. Drain noodles. In a large skillet, cook beef and onion over medium heat until meat is no longer pink; drain. Stir in spaghetti sauce and Italian seasoning. In a bowl, combine the 2 cheeses.

In a 5 quart slow cooker coated with nonstick cooking spray, spread a third of the meat sauce. Cover with a third of the noodles and pepperoni and olives (if desired). Sprinkle with a third of the cheeses. Repeat layers twice.

Cover and cook on low for 3-4 hours or until heated through and cheese is melted.

Yield: 6-8 servings

Recipe Notes

- This recipe heats up well as leftovers. Actually, my family likes the flavor better the next day.
- Almost always a hit at church dinners. I've had to share this recipe many times.
- I once took this dish to church for a family dinner after the funeral service of a local veteran. The family had invited the honor guard to stay and eat with the family. One of the young service men asked who had made this dish as he piled a large second helping onto his plate. When I met him, he told me that "this is the bomb". I looked at him a little quizzically and asked him if that was good or bad. In my generation, a "bomb" was usually a failure. I guess times have changed, he assured me that it was a "very good thing" now.

Brenda

MEXICAN CASSEROLE

Brenda Livesay

1 ½ -2 lbs ground beef
1 package of chili or taco seasoning mix
   (whatever is handy in the cabinet)
1 can mild enchilada sauce (or warmer if your
   family prefers)
1 can cream of chicken soup
1 can ranch style beans
1 cup salsa
1 lb grated cheese
1 bag of tortilla chips
   (I like to use the bite size chips)

In a large skillet, brown the ground beef until done; drain off any fat. Stir in the seasoning mix, enchilada sauce, chicken soup, beans, and salsa.

In a crock pot or large baking dish, spread a layer of tortilla chips followed by a layer of the meat mixture. Put another layer of tortilla chips and sprinkle with half the cheese. Layer the remainder of the meat sauce, another layer of chips, and sprinkle the remaining cheese on top.

If baking in an oven, cook at 350 for 20-30 minutes until it is heated through. If cooking in a crock pot, cover and cook on low for 1-2 hours.

TACO BAKE

Brenda Livesay

Taco Crust:
- 1 ¾ to 2 cups flour
- 1 package active dry yeast
- 1 tablespoon sugar
- 2 teaspoons finely chopped onion
- ¾ teaspoon salt
- 2/3 cup warm water
- 2 tablespoons oil
- ½ cup crushed taco shells or tortilla chips

Taco Meat:
- 1 lb lean ground beef
- ½ cup chopped onions
- 1 package taco seasoning mix
- ¾ cup water

Toppings:
- 1 cup shredded cheddar cheese
- 1 cup shredded lettuce
- 1 ½ cup chopped tomatoes
- Salsa and sour cream

In a medium mixing bowl, combine 1 cup flour, yeast, sugar, onion, and salt; mix well. Add very warm water (120 – 130 degrees) and oil to flour mixture. Mix by hand until almost smooth. Stir in crushed taco shells or tortilla chips and enough remaining flour to make a stiff dough. Spread in a well greased 10-inch pie pan, forming a rim around the edge. Cover; let rise in a warm place for about 20 minutes.

Meanwhile, brown the hamburger meat with the chopped onions. Add the taco seasoning and water and simmer for about 20 minutes.

Spread the meat mixture over dough. Bake at 375 degrees for 20 to 30 minutes until edge is crispy and light golden brown. Sprinkle cheese, lettuce, and tomatoes on top. Serve immediately and pass the salsa and sour cream!

PIZZA DOUGH
Brenda Livesay

1 cup warm water
1 ½ teaspoon sugar
¼ teaspoon salt
1 package yeast
1 teaspoon vegetable oil
3 cups flour

In a mixing bowl, dissolve yeast, sugar, and salt in the warm water; let stand for 15 minutes. Stir in vegetable oil and add flour one cup at a time, mixing well after each addition.

On a floured board, knead the dough until smooth (about 5-10 minutes). Cover and let rise until double. Punch down and shape onto a large well-greased baking sheet. Add desired sauce and toppings.

Bake at 400 degrees for 20-22 minutes

LIVESAY ORCHARDS BBQ CHICKEN PIZZA
Livesay Orchards

½ cup Livesay Orchards' Peach BBQ sauce
18 oz. cooked Southwestern Chicken, chopped
1 ½ cups shredded Mexican blend cheese
2 tablespoons chopped fresh cilantro
1 batch of Brenda's Pizza Dough

Prepare the pizza dough per the recipe. Bake for approximately 15 to 18 minutes in a 400 degree oven.

Spread ¼ cup of Livesay Orchards' Peach BBQ sauce over the pizza crust. Combine remaining BBQ sauce with chicken, coating well. Spoon the chicken mixture over the crust, topping with cheese and cilantro.

Bake at 450 degrees for 8 – 10 minutes, until cheese melts.

FRESH SUMMER PEACH PIZZA
Melanie Warren

1 batch of Brenda's Pizza Dough
3 tablespoons olive oil
½ teaspoon fresh basil, chopped
¼ teaspoon salt
1/8 teaspoon ground pepper
1 garlic clove, minced
6 oz. mozzarella cheese, shredded

2 large peaches, thinly sliced
¼ red onion, sliced
6 thin slices of prosciutto, cut or torn into pieces
2 oz. blue cheese
1 teaspoon balsamic vinegar
1 cup loosely packed arugula

Prepare the pizza dough per the recipe. Roll out the pizza dough into two 18 by 6 inch rectangles and place on cookie sheet sprinkled with cornmeal. I like the dough pretty thin on this recipe, so I usually try to roll it out to about ¼ inch thick. Mix together 2 tablespoons of the olive oil, chopped basil, salt, pepper, and garlic. Brush pizza crusts with the oil mixture. Add mozzarella, peaches, red onions, prosciutto, and blue cheese. Cook for 10 – 12 minutes until the crust is golden brown and the cheese is melted. Combine the balsamic vinegar, remaining 1 tablespoon of olive oil, and arugula and toss to coat. Add to the top of each pizza.

CHOCOLATE OAT CAKE
Brenda Livesay

1 cup quick-cooking or rolled oats
½ cup butter or margarine
1 ½ cups boiling water
¼ cup baking cocoa
1 cup packed brown sugar
1 cup sugar
2 eggs
1 teaspoon vanilla extract
1 ½ cups all-purpose flour
1 teaspoon salt
1 teaspoon baking soda
1 ½ cups chocolate chips
1 cup chopped nuts

Place oatmeal and butter in a large mixing bowl; pour boiling water over them and let cool for 20 minutes. Add cocoa and beat well. Beat in sugars, eggs, and vanilla. Combine flour, salt, and baking soda; add to batter. Pour into a greased 13 x 9 x 2 inch baking pan. Sprinkle with chocolate chips and nuts.

Bake at 350 degrees for 45 minutes or until cake test done.

Yield: 12-15 servings

Recipe Notes
This cake goes great with a bowl of fresh peaches!
Brenda

PECAN KISSES
Brenda Livesay

2 egg whites
1/8 teaspoon salt
2 cups sifted powdered sugar
1 teaspoon vanilla
1 teaspoon vinegar
1 ½ cups chopped pecans

In a mixing bowl, beat egg whites with salt until soft peaks form. Remember that when whipping egg whites, there should be no yolk in the whites. The fat in the yolk will hinder the whipping process and the ability to get it all light and fluffy. Gradually beat in powdered sugar, vinegar, and vanilla; continue beating until very stiff. Fold in pecans. Drop by teaspoonfuls on greased baking sheets. Bake at 300 degrees for 15 to 20 minutes or until firm (cookies remain light-colored).

Cool on racks. Makes small cookies.

Yield: about 3 ½ dozen

PEANUT BUTTER SQUARES

Brenda Livesay

1 cup flour
½ cup sugar
½ cup firmly packed brown sugar
½ teaspoon baking soda
½ teaspoon salt
½ cup margarine, softened
1/3 cup peanut butter
1 egg
1 cup quick oats, uncooked
1 package semi-sweet chocolate chips

Optional topping:
½ cup sifted powdered sugar
¼ cup creamy peanut butter
3 to 5 tablespoons of milk

Combine all ingredients, except for the chips, into a large mixing bowl and mix well. (This makes a very stiff and sticky dough and is easier if the margarine is very soft). Press the dough into a lightly greased 13x9x2 baking pan. (Makes a very thin layer). Bake at 350 degrees for 20 minutes.

Remove from oven and sprinkle with the chocolate chips immediately. Let stand for 5 minutes or until chocolate is melted; spread chocolate out evenly with a knife. Let cool before cutting.

If desired an icing to drizzle over the top can be made. Mix the ingredients together to make a thin consistency; beat well and drizzle over cookies before cutting into squares.

Recipe Notes

- Very quick and easy to make and really tastes best the day after making it. This allows the flavors to really blend and the cookie to set real well. Great dessert to make the day ahead of time for an event.
- Found this recipe in a *Progressive Farmer* magazine in January of 1982.
- Melanie has requested these cookies in place of birthday cake many times!

Brenda

SALTED NUT SQUARES
Brenda Livesay

3 cups salted peanuts without skins, divided
3 tablespoons butter or margarine
2 cups (12 ounce bag) peanut butter chips
1 can (14 ounces) sweetened condensed milk
2 cups miniature marshmallows

Place half of the peanuts in an ungreased 8 x 8 baking pan; set aside.

In a large saucepan, melt butter and peanut butter chips over low heat, stirring constantly to prevent scorching. Add milk and marshmallows; cook and stir until melted. Pour over peanuts in baking pan. Sprinkle with the remaining peanuts. Cover and refrigerate until cool. Cut into small squares.

Recipe Notes

I rarely have any of these to bring home if I take them to a gathering. Very popular with all ages. (Folks at church call them "those payday things.")

Brenda

BLACK AND BLUE COBBLER
Marsha Chasteen

1 cup all-purpose flour
1 ½ cups sugar, divided
1 teaspoon baking powder
¼ teaspoon salt
¼ teaspoon ground cinnamon
¼ teaspoon ground nutmeg
2 eggs beaten
2 tablespoons milk
2 tablespoons vegetable oil
2 cups fresh or frozen blackberries
2 cups fresh or frozen blueberries
¾ cup water
1 teaspoon grated orange peel

In a bowl, combine flour, ¾ cup sugar, baking powder, salt, cinnamon, and nutmeg. Combine eggs, milk, and oil; stir into dry ingredients just until moistened. Spread batter evenly onto the bottom of a greased 5 qt slow cooker. In a saucepan, combine berries, water, orange peel, and remaining sugar; bring to a boil. Remove from the heat; immediately pour over batter. Cover and cook on high for 2 to 2 ½ hours or until a toothpick inserted into the batter comes out clean. Turn cooker off. Uncover and let stand for 30 minutes before serving.

MIRACLE CHEESECAKE

Madeline Livesay (Kent and Steve's mother)

3 oz. package lemon Jell-O
1 cup boiling water
3 tablespoons real lemon juice
8 oz. package cream cheese
1 cup sugar
1 teaspoon vanilla
1 can chilled Milnot

Crust:
    ½ lb graham cracker crumbs
    ½ cup melted oleo

Dissolve Jell-O in boiling water. Add lemon juice and cool. Cream together cheese, sugar, and vanilla. Add to cooled Jell-O mixture. Using a mixer, whip the chilled Milnot until soft peaks form. Mix well and fold in whipped Milnot.

To make the crust, add melted butter to the fine graham cracker crumbs. Pack 2/3 of the mixture to the bottom and sides of a 9 x 13 pan. Add the filling and sprinkle the remaining crumbs on top. Chill for several hours before serving.

Recipe Notes

Kent and Steve remember their mother making these desserts many times. They are delicious, especially served with fresh peaches or blackberries!

BUTTERMILK POUND CAKE

Madeline Livesay

3 cups sugar
1 cup Crisco
6 eggs, separated
1 teaspoon vanilla
2 teaspoons butter flavoring
2 teaspoons lemon extract
3 cups flour
½ teaspoon salt
¼ teaspoon baking soda
1 cup buttermilk
1 stick butter, melted

Mix sugar and Crisco well. Add egg yolks to the mixture one at a time, blending well after each egg is added. Add vanilla, butter flavoring, and lemon extract.

Sift flour, salt, and baking soda together. Add the dry ingredients and the buttermilk to the sugar/Crisco mixture, alternating between the dry ingredients and the milk, mixing well after each addition. When you are alternating between the dry ingredients and the milk, begin and end with the dry ingredients.

Beat the egg whites until stiff. Carefully fold into the mixture (do this by hand and very gently so you don't stir out the "fluffiness" of the egg whites.

Pour in a 10-inch tube pan that has been greased and floured. Bake at 350 degrees for about 1 hour and 10 minutes, until a toothpick inserted in the center comes out clean.

Pour 1 tablespoon of melted butter over the hot cake and serve warm.

BLACKBERRY PIE BARS
Livesay Orchards

3 cups flour
1 ½ cups sugar, divided
1 teaspoon baking powder
1 teaspoon cinnamon
¼ teaspoon salt
1 lemon
2 sticks cold unsalted butter
1 egg
2 teaspoons vanilla extract
1 quart fresh Livesay Orchards blackberries
4 teaspoons cornstarch

Mix together the flour, 1 cup of sugar, baking powder, cinnamon, and salt in a food processor. Add some zest from the lemon. Add the butter, egg, and vanilla extract to the processor. Cut together until the dough is crumbly. Pat half of the dough into the bottom of a 13x9 inch greased pan, saving the remaining dough for the topping.

In a medium bowl, stir together the remaining ½ cup sugar, cornstarch, and the juice from one lemon. Gently mix in the blackberries. Sprinkle the blackberry mixture evenly over the crust. Crumble the remaining dough over the berries.

Bake at 375 degrees for about 45 minutes, until the top is slightly brown. Cool completely and then cut into 12 bars.

SLOW COOKER BLACKBERRY COBBLER
Livesay Orchards

2 cup milk
2 cup flour
2 ½ cups sugar, divided
1 stick (½ cup) melted butter
1 quart Livesay Orchard blackberries

Mix together milk, flour, 2 cups of sugar, and the melted butter. Pour in a crock-pot that has been liberally sprayed with non-stick cooking spray. Add the blackberries on top of this mixture, spreading them out evenly over the flour mixture. Sprinkle the remaining ½ cup of sugar on top. Cover and cook for 2 – 2 ½ hours on high. It is mandatory that you serve this goodness with vanilla ice cream!

PECAN PIE BARS
Melanie Warren

2/3 cup granulated sugar
½ cup butter, softened
2 teaspoon vanilla extract, divided
1 ½ cups flour
2/3 cup packed brown sugar
½ cup dark corn syrup
¼ teaspoon salt
3 eggs
1 cup coarsely chopped pecans

Lightly grease the bottom and sides of a 13x9 inch pan with shortening or spray well with cooking spray. In a large bowl, mix the granulated sugar, butter, and 1 teaspoon of vanilla. Stir in flour. Press dough in the bottom and about ½ inch up the side of the pan. Bake 15 to 17 minutes in a 350 degree oven or until the edges are light brown.

Meanwhile, in a medium bowl, beat the brown sugar, corn syrup, the other teaspoon of vanilla, the salt, and eggs with a spoon. Stir in the pecans. Pour over crust. Bake 25 to 30 minutes or until the mixture is set up. Loosen the edges from the sides of the pan while warm. Cool completely, about an hour. Cut into bars.

I got this recipe from a Betty Crocker pamphlet several years ago. The original recipe called for melting semisweet chocolate chips and dipping one end of each bar into the melted chocolate, laying flat on waxed paper to dry. But, these never last long enough at my house to get dipped all pretty!

INDEX

PEACH RECIPES:

5 Minute Peach Frozen Yogurt 29
5 Minute Peach Mug Cake 28
Chicken with Grilled Peaches and Arugula 31
Creamy Peach Pie 24
Crockpot Peach BBQ Beef 33
Foolproof Piecrust 22
Fresh Peach Pie 22
Glazed Peach Pie 22
Grilled Chicken with Peach Salsa 35
Grilled Peaches and Gelato 35
Homemade Peach Ice Cream 29
Honey Peach Butter 12
Kaylee's Peach Salsa 35
Mel's Famous Peach Milkshakes 14
Peaches and Cream Cake 17
Peach and Blackberry Pie 23
Peach and Blueberry Coffee Cake 18
Peach Basil Chicken Salad 31
Peach Breakfast Parfaits 30
Peach Cobbler 26
Peach Crisp 20
Peach Crumble 21
Peach Dessert Enchiladas 21
Peach Freezer Jam 12
Peach Glazed Pork Chops 34
Peach Iced Tea 14
Peach Jalapeño Pepper Jelly 13
Peach Jell-O Pie 24
Peach Melba Float 14
Peach Muffins 16
Peach Pepper Vinaigrette 13
Peach Pound Cake 17
Peach Roll Ups 21
Peach Salsa Nachos 33
Peach Slush 14
Peaches and Cream Gelatin 30
Peachy Pizza 30
Pecan Peach Cobbler 27
Porter Peach BBQ Ribs 34
Quick and Easy Hand Pies 22
Roasted Peaches 33
Sugar Substitute Peach Cobbler 28

APPLE RECIPES:

Apple Butter 42
Apple Danish 51
Apple Fritters 53
Apple Nut Cake 50
Apple Pie Poke Cake 52
Apple Raisin Bread 44
Apples and Homemade Salted Caramel Sauce 47
Blackberry Apple Jelly 43
Chocolate Apple Cake 53
Crockpot Apple Cider 46
Dawna's Apple Salad 48
Easy Apple Dumplings 54
English Apple Pie 54
Fresh Apple Cake 50
Fried Apples 49
Honeyed Apple Treat 55
Pork Chops and Fried Apples 49
Streusel-Topped Apple Muffins 45
Taffy Apple Salad 48

PUMPKIN RECIPES:

Chocolate Pumpkin Snickerdoodles 62
Cranberry Pumpkin Bread............................ 59
Maple Pumpkin Muffins................................. 58
Pumpkin and Chocolate Chip Oat Bars ... 63
Pumpkin and Pecan Cheesecake 64
Pumpkin Bread 59
Pumpkin Chocolate Chip Muffins 58
Pumpkin Cinnamon Rolls............................. 60
Pumpkin Cookies... 62
Pumpkin Dip 63

FARM FRIENDLY RECIPES:

5 Day Sweet Pickles 68
Baked Squash 72
Baked Summer Squash with Cheese........... 72
Black and Blue Cobbler 82
Blackberry Pie Bars.. 84
Broccoli Rice Casserole 74
Buttermilk Pound Cake 83
Cantaloupe Fresca 69
Cheeseburger Cups.. 75
Chocolate Oak Cake 80
Crockpot Pizza 76
Favorite Fruit Punch 69
Fresh Summer Peach Pizza........................... 79
Hashbrown Casserole................................... 75
Livesay Orchards BBQ Chicken Pizza........ 79
Macaroni Salad 72
Marinated Tomato Salad 72
Mexican Casserole... 77
Miracle Cheesecake....................................... 83
No-Knead Refrigerator Rolls 73
Peanut Butter Squares 81
Pecan Kisses 80
Pecan Pie Bars... 85
Pizza Dough... 79
Salted Nut Squares 82
Slow Cooker Blackberry Cobbler............... 84
Southwest Grilled Chicken 71
Spanish Rice... 74
Spicy Grilled Melons 71
Taco Bake 78
Watermelon Sweet and Spicy Salsa 71

Sam Davis, hobbyist pilot, local pastor, and friend, took this photo from his plane one summer day in 2012, showing part of the original 462-acre farm as well as the orchard to the north of the original farm which was purchased from the Thomas family in 1977.

Made in the USA
Charleston, SC
05 September 2016